Dear f
Here ꞏrꞏies
to read ne .
This can be a help to them to
learn more of the Bible.
Read one story each evening and
ask them the questions or discuss
them together.
Justus & Emma Kulp
270-427-2400

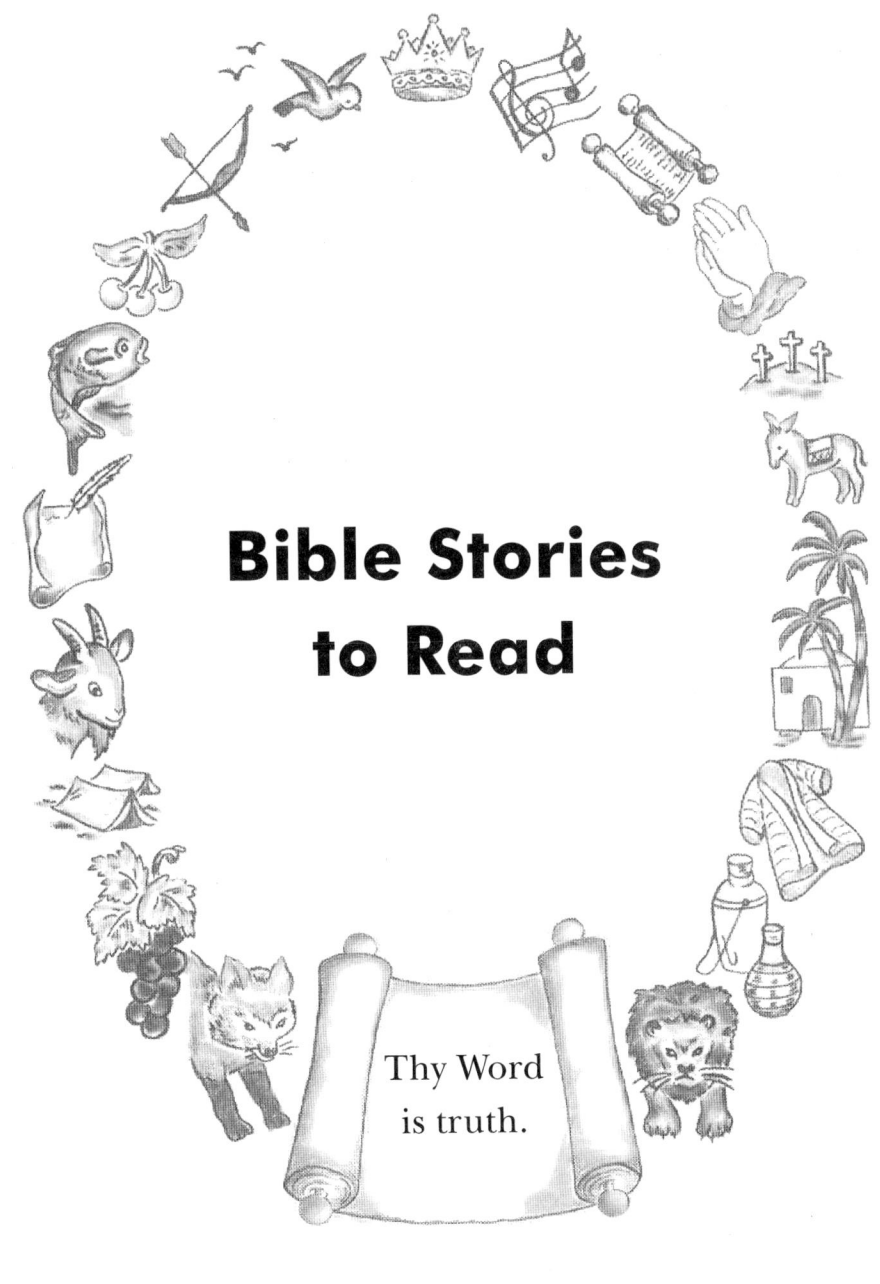

Bible Stories
to Read

Thy Word
is truth.

Bible Stories to Read

Written and illustrated by Martha Rohrer

Acknowledgements

We acknowledge God who has given to us His Word. The writer wishes to express her gratitude to many teachers, ministers, and writers, as well as her family, who have shared the precious truths of the Bible. We appreciate the contributions of various brethren and sisters who have assisted in editing and reviewing these lessons.

—The Publishers

Copyright 1989

Rod and Staff Publishers, Inc.
Crockett, Kentucky 41413

Telephone (606) 522-4348

Printed in USA

ISBN 978-07399-0021-5

Catalog no. 10002

26   27   28   29   30   —   31   30   29   28   27   26   25   24   23   22

Dedicated to
    my mother
who regularly read
Bible stories to all
her children.

Message to Parents

Children love stories told or read over and over. These stories are chosen to give an introduction to the Bible from Genesis to Revelation.

We have tried to keep the stories Biblically accurate. Although many Bible characters were not perfect heroes, God helped them when they were faithful. God's promises are true today as well. Obedience brings His blessing, and disobedience brings judgment. We also recognize His love to all in sending rain and natural blessings upon the just and the unjust.

The stories have been kept brief and simple, but the reader may desire to add explanations or more Bible details at his discretion.

Good stories help to develop your child's character. Point out the exact Bible passage upon which the story is based. Guide your child's faith by a sincere belief and appreciation for His Word in your own heart.

Reading in a conversational tone, pausing at a moment of suspense, reading fast or slow according to the sense of the story, and using gestures in a natural way help make the story alive and delightful to little listeners. We want the child's attention span to increase and his comprehension to develop. But most of all, we want the child's love and understanding of God and the Bible to grow.

How to use *Bible Stories to Read* with *Bible Pictures to Color*

The child should be taught to sit quietly and listen as the parent reads the Bible story to him. Ask the child questions about the story, and discuss the corresponding picture before giving the child the opportunity to color the picture carefully.

A few questions are included with each story, but the parent is encouraged to discuss the story further, adding more questions of his own. Reread parts of the story if necessary to help the child think of the answers. Questions that begin with *who, what, when, where, why,* and *how* help to increase the child's comprehension and vocabulary. The child should learn to tell who or what each picture shows.

The verse may be learned and reviewed throughout the day at various times. Repetition is vital for lasting memorization.

Table of Contents

Old Testament

New Testament

"The Lord our God will we serve, and his voice will we obey."   *Joshua 24:24*

"For ever, O Lord, thy word is settled in heaven."   *Psalm 119:89*

"O how love I thy law!"   *Psalm 119:97*

"Read in the roll . . . the words of the Lord."   *Jeremiah 36:6*

Old

Testament

1. The Bible Is From God

2 Peter 1:20, 21

We are glad God gave us the Bible. We call it God's Word because it tells us the things He wants us to know. God wants us to know that He made us. He wants us to know how to do what is right and how to worship Him. God wants us to know about heaven. He wants us to know that we can live with Him in heaven after we die. Everything the Bible tells us is true.

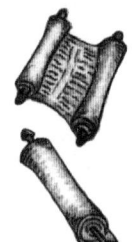

God wants us to know so many things that we cannot remember them all. But He told holy men to write His message. These men listened and wrote just what God said. The words they wrote are in the Bible. Now we can read it and learn it. We can read it again and again. God wants us to obey it too.

Many years ago there were not books with pages like we have today. Often scribes copied the Bible words on scrolls for the people to read. A scroll was made from a long, long piece of parchment, or paper, that was rolled on a stick. When a person read the scroll, he would roll it from one stick to another stick.

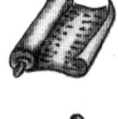

Sometimes God's people did not do what the Bible said. They did not even want to hear the Bible words. Then God punished them. He wants all people to hear and obey His Word.

We are glad our parents read the Bible stories to us today. We want to listen quietly and hear God's words at home and at church. We want to learn more about God and obey Him.

We can sing about the Bible too. Here is a song for you to sing.

I have a wonderful treasure, The gift of God without measure,

And so we travel together,   My Bible and I.

Questions and Answers

1. Who gave us the Bible?

   God gave us the Bible.

2. What does the Bible tell us?

   (Various answers are correct.)

3. Should we be glad to hear the Bible stories?

   Yes, we should be glad.

Bible Verse to Learn
"Thy word is truth." John 17:17

2. God Created the World

Long ago there was no beautiful world. There were no people. There was just darkness.

God was in heaven. He saw the darkness, and He made the earth and sky. He made it all out of nothing. He made everything in six days.

God just spoke the word, and whatever He said was made. He said, "Let there be light," and there was light. God called the light day, and the darkness He called night. That was the very first day.

The next day God spoke and made the beautiful blue sky. He made the fluffy clouds in the sky.

Then He told the waters to gather in certain places on the third day. In this way He made the dry land between the streams, the rivers, and the oceans. But nothing grew on the land. So God spoke and made the plants. Green grass and pretty flowers and vegetables grew. Bushes with berries and trees with fruit grew. Everything was good, but God was not finished.

He spoke on the next day, and the sun shone in the blue sky. The moon and stars shone at night. The earth and sky were beautiful in the daytime and at night.

On the fifth day God made the fish and the birds. Great sharks and small goldfish went swimming through the water. Bright red cardinals and tiny hummingbirds flew about. Owls and peacocks and doves appeared.

At last on the sixth day, God spoke once more and made the animals. There were big, gray elephants and small chipmunks. There were many, many different animals, but there were still no people.

Then God took some dust of the earth and made a man. He breathed into the man, and the man became a living soul. God called the man Adam. God knew that the man needed a helper. So God made Adam sleep. God took a bone out of Adam and made a woman to help him.

God looked at everything that He had made. It was all very good. On the seventh day, God rested. He had finished creating the beautiful world.

Questions and Answers

1. What happened when God spoke?

   The things He said were made.

2. What did God make to shine at night?

   God made the moon and stars to shine at night.

3. Who did God make out of dust?

   God made Adam out of dust.

Bible Verse to Learn

"God created the heaven and the earth." Genesis 1:1

3. Adam and Eve Sin

God planted a beautiful garden called Eden. A sparkling river watered the plants. Adam and his wife, Eve, lived in this lovely garden. God told them to care for the garden and to eat its fruit.

But there was one tree in the middle of the garden that God said, "You shall not eat from this one tree or you will die."

Adam and Eve were very happy. They loved God. They walked and

talked with God when the day was cool. They took care of the plants in the garden and ate the good food. They did what God wanted them to do.

But one day a very sad thing happened. Satan came and talked to Eve. Satan was in a snake. Satan said, "Did God tell you not to eat of every tree of the garden?"

Eve answered, "We may eat of all the trees except one. God said that if we eat of it or touch it, we will die."

Then Satan told Eve a lie. He said, "You will not die. God knows that if you eat of this tree, you will be wise and know what is right and wrong."

Now Eve looked at that one tree. The fruit looked good. She wanted to be wise. So she picked some fruit and ate it. She gave some to Adam, and he ate it too.

But they had disobeyed God. They had done what God said they should not do. Now they felt very bad. They did not want to walk and talk with God because they were afraid. So they hid among the trees in the garden.

But God knew where they were. He came and talked to them. He asked them what they did. He needed to punish them. He told them they would have to work hard for their food. They would have pain and trouble, and someday Adam and Eve would have to die. God put them out of the garden.

Adam and Eve had brought sin into God's beautiful world. But God still loved them. He made coats of animal skins for them to wear. He gave them a wonderful promise. Someday God would send a Saviour into the world to take away their sin.

Questions and Answers

1. Who lived in a beautiful garden?
   Adam and Eve lived in a beautiful garden.

2. Who told Adam and Eve a lie?
   Satan in a snake told Adam and Eve a lie.

3. Was God pleased when Adam and Eve disobeyed?
   No, God needed to punish them.

Bible Verse to Learn
"We ought to obey God." Acts 5:29

4. Cain and Abel Grow Up

God gave Adam and Eve a baby boy. They named him Cain. This made Eve very happy. After a time Cain had a baby brother named Abel.

When Cain grew up, he became a farmer. He planted seeds in the ground and took care of the plants as they grew. When the crops were ready, Cain picked them.

When Abel grew up, he took care of sheep. He fed and watered the sheep each day.

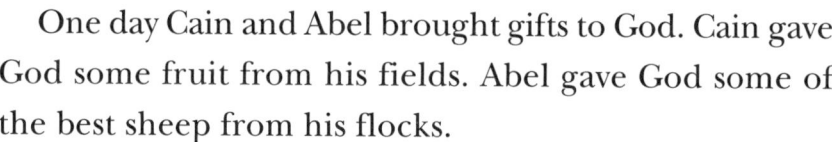

One day Cain and Abel brought gifts to God. Cain gave God some fruit from his fields. Abel gave God some of the best sheep from his flocks.

God was pleased with Abel's gift, but He was not pleased with Cain's gift. Then Cain became very angry.

God said to Cain, "If you will obey Me, I will accept your gift."

But Cain did not obey God. Instead, he began to hate Abel.

One day when they were together in the field, Cain was so angry that he killed Abel.

Then God asked Cain, "Where is your brother Abel?"

Cain was not honest. He told God, "I do not know. Must I take care of my brother?"

God knew what Cain had done. God said, "Your brother is dead. Because you killed him, you must be punished. When you work in the fields, the plants will not grow well. You will move from one place to another all your life."

Now Cain did not have a home. His crops would not grow well. He said, "My punishment is too hard. Everyone who sees me will try to kill me."

Then God put a mark on Cain. People knew they should not kill Cain when they saw that mark.

God gave Adam and Eve another son in place of Abel. They called the new baby Seth.

Adam lived a long, long time. He lived nine hundred thirty years. He had many children. God blessed Adam and Eve and their children on the earth.

Questions and Answers

1. What did Abel do when he grew up?
   Abel took care of sheep.

2. Which son did not obey God?
   Cain did not obey God.

3. How did Abel die?
   Cain killed his brother Abel.

Bible Verse to Learn

"Love one another." John 15:12

5. Noah and the Flood

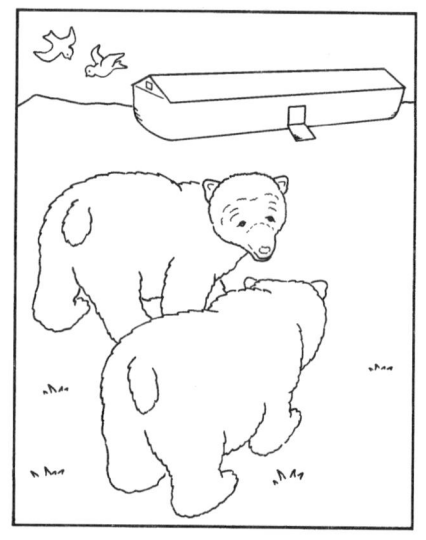

After a time there were many, many people on the earth. But most of the people were bad. Every day they sinned more and more.

This made God feel sorry. He said, "I will punish all the wicked people."

But one man loved God. His name was Noah. God wanted to save Noah and his family.

God said to Noah, "I will destroy the wicked people. I want you to make a big boat because I am going to send a flood on the earth. All the wicked people will die, but you and your family will be safe inside the big boat. Also you will take birds and animals of every kind into the boat. Put in food too. Put in enough food to last a long time for your family and for the animals."

Noah believed God. He did everything just as God said he should. Noah's three sons helped him. It took them many years to build the big, strong boat. The boat was called an ark. At last it was finished.

Then the food was put in the ark. Also the birds and the animals went into the ark. Some animals went in two by two, and some went in seven by seven just as God said.

When Noah's family and the animals were in the ark, God shut the door.

Soon it began to rain. It rained and rained for forty days. The water became deeper and deeper until it covered all the mountains. All the wicked people were drowned. Only Noah's family were safe in the ark.

After many, many days, the water began to go down. At last the ground was dry. Noah and his family and all the animals came out of the ark.

Noah built an altar and worshiped God. God made a promise to Noah. He said, "I will never again send a flood on the earth to destroy all the people."

God put a beautiful rainbow in the sky. He told Noah, "Every time you see My rainbow in the sky, I want you to remember My promise." God has always kept His promise, and we know He always will.

Questions and Answers

1. Who loved God?

   Noah loved God.

2. What did God tell Noah to build?

   God told Noah to build an ark.

3. What did God put in the sky?

   God put a rainbow in the sky.

Bible Verse to Learn

"By faith Noah . . . prepared an ark." Hebrews 11:7

6. Abraham Has Faith in God

After the flood, Noah's sons had children. Soon there were many people on the earth again. At that time all the people talked in one language. But many people did not worship God.

They said, "Let's make a high tower that will reach to heaven. We want everyone to know who we are. We will be great men."

So they started to build, but God was not pleased. He made the people speak different languages. Many people moved far away because they could not understand each other.

Some time after this, God talked to a man named Abram. God said, "I want you to move away from your father's land. I want you to go to a land that I will show you. I will bless your family greatly, and your family will be a blessing to all the people on the earth. Someday the Saviour will be born from your children."

Abram believed God. He and his wife moved to the land of Canaan as God had said they should. Abram's nephew Lot went with them. In the land of Canaan, Abram built an altar and worshiped God. God said to Abram, "I will give this land to your children." It was a very good land, and God blessed Abram there.

But Abram and his wife still did not have any children. So Abram asked God how He would bless his family. God told Abram to look up at the sky at night. God asked, "Can you count all the stars? I will bless your family so that your children's children will be more than you can count."

When Abram was an old man, God changed his name to Abraham. God again promised Abraham many blessings.

All this time Abraham believed God even though he had no children. Now God said Abraham and Sarah would have a baby boy.

God kept His promise. When Abraham was one hundred years old, Baby Isaac was born. This made Abraham and Sarah very happy. They took good care of Baby Isaac. They taught him to love and worship God.

Questions and Answers

1. Who told Abram to move away from his father's land?
   God told Abram to move.

2. Who believed all God's promises?
   Abraham (Abram) believed all God's promises.

3. Who was born when Abraham was very old?
   Baby Isaac was born when Abraham was old.

Bible Verse to Learn

"Abraham believed God." Romans 4:3

7. Lot Chooses the Best Pastures

When Abraham moved to Canaan, his nephew Lot went with him. Abraham had many sheep and cattle and tents. Lot also had many sheep and cattle and tents. They had servants to take care of all their many animals.

But sometimes the servants quarreled. They needed plenty of green pasture for all the animals. They needed fresh water too.

Abraham wanted to help the men. Abraham said to Lot, "There is enough land for both of us. We do not want our workers to quarrel and fight. You may choose the fields you want, and I will take my animals and men to other fields."

Lot looked at the many fields. He did not want the hilly pastures. He liked the green pastures near the river. So Lot chose the best pastures for himself. Then Lot moved close to two very wicked cities.

After Lot had moved, God said to Abraham, "Look around you in every direction. I will give all this land to you and your children."

Abraham believed God. He moved to new pastures. There Abraham built an altar and worshiped God.

Lot had moved to the best land, but things did not go well for him and his family.

Lot moved his family right into one of the wicked cities. One time some enemies came. They took Lot and some other people away. Then Abraham was kind. Abraham and his men rescued Lot and the other people.

The people in the two cities were very wicked. So God said He would burn those cities with fire. God sent two angels to tell Lot and his family to get out. But Lot did not go. Finally the angels led Lot and his wife and two daughters out of the city. The angels said, "Go quickly to the mountain. Do not look back." But Lot's wife looked back. She became a pillar of salt.

Lot had many troubles because he did not always choose God's best way. But Abraham was happy. He worshiped and obeyed God. Abraham was a peacemaker.

Questions and Answers

1. Who had many animals?

   Abraham and Lot had many animals.

2. Who chose the best pastures for himself?

   Lot chose the best pastures for himself.

3. Who always worshiped God wherever he moved?

   Abraham always worshiped God.

Bible Verse to Learn

"Blessed are the peacemakers." Matthew 5:9

8. Isaac Is Offered

Abraham and Sarah's son Isaac grew. They loved him very much.

God saw how Abraham loved Isaac, and God gave Abraham a very hard test. God said, "Take your son to a certain mountain. Lay him on an altar and kill him there to offer him to Me."

Abraham wanted to do whatever God said, so he got up early in the morning. He took Isaac and two young men with him. They started to go to the place God told him. After traveling three days, Abraham could see the mountain far away.

Abraham said to the two men, "Stay here and wait. We will come back to you."

Then Isaac carried the wood, and Abraham took the fire and a knife. They went on together.

As they were walking, Isaac asked, "Father, we have fire and wood, but where is the lamb to offer to God?"

Abraham answered his son kindly, "My son, God will have a lamb ready for the offering."

Abraham and Isaac kept walking. Isaac trusted his father. When they came to the right place, Abraham built an altar. He put the wood on it. Then he laid his only son

Isaac on the wood. Abraham took the knife in his hand to kill his son.

Just then the angel of the Lord called from heaven, "Abraham! Abraham!"

Abraham answered, "Here am I."

The angel said, "Do not harm your son. Now I am sure that you fear God because you were ready to give your son when God asked for him."

Abraham looked behind him. A sheep was caught in the bushes by his horns. Abraham took the sheep and offered it on the altar to God instead of his son.

Then the angel called to Abraham again. He said, "God will bless you and your children greatly, and others shall be blessed because you loved and obeyed God."

How happy Abraham was! He trusted God and believed God's promises. Abraham loved God most of all.

Questions and Answers

1. Did Abraham love his only son?

   Yes, Abraham loved his only son.

2. Did Abraham kill his only son?

   No, Abraham did not kill his only son.

3. Whom did Abraham love most of all?

   Abraham loved God most of all.

Bible Verse to Learn
"I will love thee, O Lord." Psalm 18:1

9. Jacob and Esau Are Twins

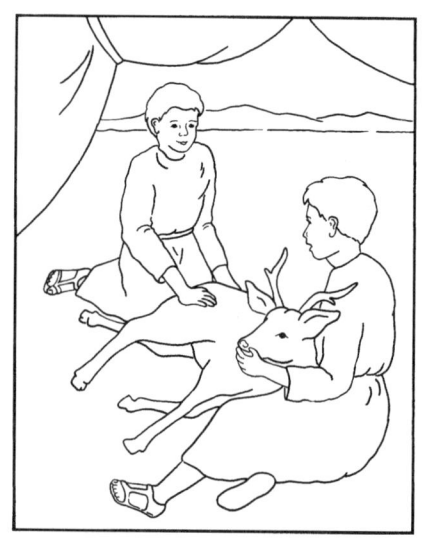

When Isaac was a man, Abraham sent his servant to find the right wife for Isaac. The servant prayed, and God helped him bring Rebekah to be Isaac's wife. Isaac loved his wife Rebekah.

God gave Isaac and Rebekah twin boys. Esau was older, and Jacob was the younger twin. Esau liked to hunt wild animals, but Jacob enjoyed helping near the tents.

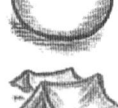

Isaac had many, many animals. His animals needed green pastures and water. When some men wanted to use his wells to water their animals, Isaac just moved away and dug more wells. Isaac did not quarrel. He wanted to be a peacemaker like his father, Abraham, had been. God promised to bless Isaac and his children just as God had promised to bless Abraham.

Isaac was growing old. Before he died, he wanted to give Esau a special blessing. He told Esau to bring some delicious venison to him. Then Isaac would bless Esau.

But while Esau went hunting, Rebekah helped Jacob. She wanted Jacob to get the good blessing. So she prepared some meat for Jacob to give to Isaac. Isaac was blind, so he did not know it was Jacob who had brought the meat. Isaac blessed Jacob before Esau came home.

This made Esau very sad and angry. He said, "When my father dies, I will kill Jacob."

After this, Jacob was sent away to find a good wife. One night while Jacob slept, he dreamed that he saw a high ladder. It reached from earth to heaven. Angels were going up and down on the ladder. God stood at the top. God said to Jacob, "I will be with you. I will bless you and your children and give you this land."

When Jacob awoke, he worshiped God. He promised to obey God. Then Jacob went on his way to his Uncle Laban's house. There Jacob married and had a family.

It was many, many years before Jacob brought his family home to his father and to his brother Esau. Esau was not angry anymore. God kept His promise. God was with Jacob and blessed him.

Questions and Answers

1. Who was Isaac's wife?

   Rebekah was Isaac's wife.

2. Who were Isaac's twin boys?

   Esau and Jacob were Isaac's twin boys.

3. Who dreamed about a high ladder and the angels?

   Jacob dreamed about a ladder and angels.

Bible Verse to Learn

"Be ye kind one to another." Ephesians 4:32

10. Joseph and His Dreams

Jacob had twelve sons, but he loved Joseph more than the other sons. Jacob gave Joseph a beautiful coat of many colors. This made the older brothers hate Joseph.

One day Joseph said to his brothers, "I dreamed we were working in a field. My bundle of wheat stood up, and your bundles bowed to my bundle." His brothers did not want to bow to Joseph. They hated him even more than before.

Joseph dreamed again. He told his brothers and his father, "This time the sun and moon and eleven stars bowed to me." His brothers did not want to hear this, but his father wondered if the dreams would come true.

One time Jacob said to Joseph, "I want you to go to your older brothers. See how they are getting along, and come back and tell me."

Joseph obeyed his father. His brothers were far from home, but Joseph kept looking until he found them.

The brothers were caring for their father's animals. They saw Joseph coming. They said, "Here comes the dreamer. Let's kill him."

But Reuben, the oldest brother, said, "Do not kill him.

Just put him into a deep hole." Reuben wanted to save Joseph and send him home when his brothers were not near.

So the brothers took off Joseph's coat. They put him into the deep hole. Then they sat down to eat.

Soon a group of men on camels came riding by. These men bought and sold many things. Judah had an idea. He said, "Let's sell Joseph to these men." So the brothers sold Joseph for twenty pieces of money. They hated Joseph so much they did not care what happened to him.

Reuben was not there at that time. When he returned, he was very sad. The brothers put blood on Joseph's coat and took it home to their father. They said, "We found this." Their father thought a wild animal had killed his son Joseph. Jacob cried and cried.

All this time Joseph was taken farther and farther away. But God was with Joseph and took care of him.

Questions and Answers

1. Who told about his dreams?

   Joseph told about his dreams.

2. Did a wild animal kill Joseph?

   No, a wild animal did not kill Joseph.

3. Who cried and cried when Joseph did not come home?

   Joseph's father, Jacob, cried and cried.

Bible Verse to Learn

"He careth for you." 1 Peter 5:7

11. Joseph's Dreams Come True

The men who bought Joseph took him to the land of Egypt. There he was sold to a rich man. Joseph was a very good worker, but the man's wife told lies about Joseph. The man believed his wife and put Joseph into prison.

Even in prison, Joseph was a good worker. He helped take care of the other prisoners.

One night two prisoners had dreams. God helped Joseph to know

what the dreams meant. The dreams both came true.

After two more years, the king had dreams, but no one could tell him what they meant. Then one man remembered Joseph in prison. The king said, "Bring him to me."

They quickly brought Joseph. He listened to the king tell his dreams. Then Joseph said, "God gave you the dreams. There will be seven good years when much food

will grow. After that will come seven bad years when little or nothing will grow. You should find a wise man to help the people save all the food they can in the good years so there will be food to eat in the bad years."

The king was pleased. He said, "There is no man as wise as you are. You will be the ruler." The king gave

Joseph fine clothes, and everyone had to bow to Joseph
and obey him. Joseph helped the people save much food.

Then the bad years came. Many, many people came from
far away to buy food in Egypt. One day Joseph's brothers
came. They bowed to Joseph, but they did not know that
the ruler was their brother. Joseph did not tell them who
he was. He gave them food, and they went home.

The next time they came, Joseph told them who he
was. Now they were afraid. They thought Joseph would
punish them for the bad things they had done. But Joseph
cried and kissed them. He was not angry. Joseph said,
"There will be five more bad years. Hurry and bring my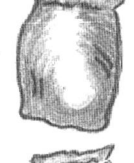
father and your families to Egypt. You may live in the best
part of the land, and I will take care of you."

Jacob was so glad to see his son Joseph again. God was
with Joseph and made his dreams come true.

Questions and Answers

1. Who helped the people save food?
   Joseph helped the people save food.

2. Did Joseph's brothers bow to him?
   Yes, his brothers bowed to him.

3. Was Joseph angry with his brothers?
   No, he was not angry. He was kind to them.

Bible Verse to Learn
"The Lord was with Joseph." Genesis 39:2

12. Job Worships God

In the land of Uz lived a rich man named Job. Job worshiped God. One time when Satan talked to God, God asked Satan, "Do you see how Job obeys Me?"

Satan replied, "Job serves You only because You give him many good things. If You take away his riches, Job would curse You."

God said to Satan, "You may take his things away from him."

So Satan gave Job many troubles.  All his oxen, donkeys, and camels were stolen. Fire burned his sheep. And saddest of all, a great wind made the house fall on Job's children. They all died.

But Job did not curse God. He blessed God.

Satan came to God again. God asked, "Have you seen how Job still loves and obeys Me?"

Satan said, "If You hurt him, Job will not love You."

God said, "You may hurt Job, but do not kill him."

So Satan gave Job sore boils all over his body. Job was very, very miserable, but he did not curse God.

Three of Job's friends came to visit him. They saw that 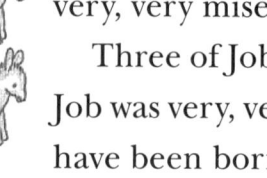 Job was very, very sad. At last Job said, "I wish I would not have been born. My troubles are so great."

His friends said, "Job, you must have done wrong, and God is punishing you. Please say you are sorry for your sin so God will take your troubles away."

But Job answered, "God knows that I helped the needy people and made them happy. Men listened to my advice. But now even young people make fun of me."

The friends talked to Job a long time. They thought surely Job had been bad. And Job thought he had tried to do right. So they stopped talking together.

Then God talked to Job from a whirlwind. God asked Job many questions. Job felt very small.

God said to Job's friends, "What you told Job was not right. Ask Job to pray so I will not punish you."

Then God gave Job many more riches. God gave him twice as many animals as he had had before. God gave him more children. Job blessed God, and God was pleased.

Questions and Answers

1. Who gave Job many troubles?

   Satan gave Job many troubles.

2. Who came to visit Job?

   Job's friends came to visit Job.

3. Was God pleased with Job?

   Yes, God was pleased with Job.

Bible Verse to Learn

"Blessed be the name of the Lord." Job 1:21

13. Baby Moses in the Boat

When Jacob and his sons moved to Egypt, Joseph and the king were kind to them. God had changed Jacob's name to Israel, so all his children were called the children of Israel.

After many, many years, there was a new king in Egypt who did not remember Joseph. The new king saw the children of Israel, and he was afraid. He said, "These people are strong, and there are so many of them. We must make their work so hard for them that they will become weak."

So the cruel king made the children of Israel work very hard. But God helped them become stronger.

Then the king said, "All the baby boys of the children of Israel must be thrown into the river."

The families loved their babies. So one of the families tried to hide their baby boy. His mother made a small boat that no water could get in. Then she put the baby in the boat. She put the boat among the plants at the edge of the water. The baby's big sister stayed close enough to watch the baby.

After a time the princess and her maids came to the

river. They saw the small boat. When they looked inside, the baby started to cry. The princess loved the baby. She wanted to save him.

Soon his sister came near. She said, "Shall I find a woman to take care of the baby?"

When the princess said yes, the baby's sister went to bring their own mother. The princess said, "Please take care of this baby for me, and I will pay you." The princess named him Moses. How happy his family was because God helped them to save their baby!

When Moses was older, he went to live with the princess. He lived in a fine house. He had fine clothes and fine food, but he never forgot his own people, the children of Israel. He saw how hard they had to work, and he wanted to help them. God wanted Moses to lead His people, so God told Moses what to do.

Questions and Answers

1. Where did Moses' mother hide the baby?

   She hid him in a small boat on the river.

2. Who stayed near to watch the baby?

   His sister stayed near to watch the baby.

3. Who had to work very hard?

   The children of Israel had to work very hard.

Bible Verse to Learn

"The Lord is my helper." Hebrews 13:6

14. Moses Leads God's People

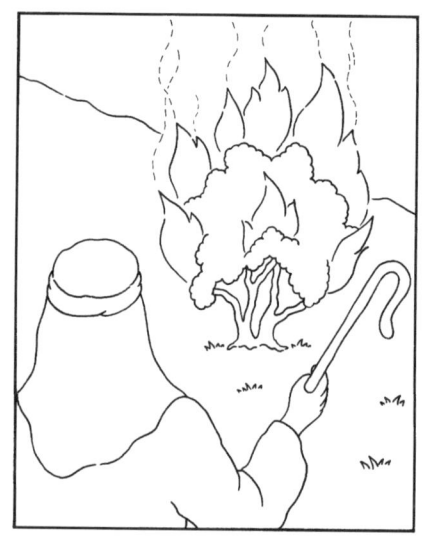

Before Moses was ready to lead God's people, God needed to teach Moses what to do. Moses lived in the wilderness for forty years. There he had a wife and children.

One day when Moses was caring for the sheep, he saw a bush that kept burning and burning. God talked to Moses from the burning bush. God said, "I want you to go back to Egypt. I know My people have to work very, very hard. I want you to lead them to the land of Canaan to live."

So Moses went back to Egypt and did just what God said. Moses and his brother Aaron went to the king. They said, "God wants you to let the children of Israel go to serve Him."

The king said, "I do not know your God, and I will not let your people go." The king did not know who would do the hard work if the children of Israel left his land. So now he made them work even harder.

God saw how cruel the king was. God sent many troubles upon the king and the people of Egypt. But after each trouble, the king would not let the people go. God sent frogs, and lice, and sickness, and hail, and other troubles. The land was dark even in the daytime. But still the king would not let God's people go.

Last of all, one night God made the oldest child die in every family in Egypt. But not one child of Israel died because God's people put blood from lambs on their doorposts as God had said. Then the king said to Moses, "Go quickly before your God kills all of us."

Moses and all the children of Israel were ready to go. They left Egypt and came to the Red Sea. But then the king changed his mind. He came after them to bring them back to his land.

Then God did a wonderful thing. He made a dry path right through the water for Moses to lead His people. When the king and his men followed, God made the water cover them, and they were all drowned. God can do wonderful things when His people trust and obey Him.

Questions and Answers

1. How did the children of Israel have to work?
   They had to work very, very hard.

2. Who did God want to lead His people?
   God wanted Moses to lead His people.

3. Did Moses and God's people drown in the Red Sea?
   No, they went on the dry path.

Bible Verse to Learn
"O Lord, how great are thy works!" Psalm 92:5

15. God's People Travel

After Moses and God's people left the Red Sea, they came to the wilderness. They were on their way to the Promised Land.

God helped them at all times. He showed them the way to go. In the daytime, when God's cloud moved, the people carried their tents. At night the cloud of fire gave them light.

When they had only bad water, God made it good. When they had no water to drink, God gave them water out of a rock.

When the people were hungry, God sent manna each morning to make bread. He sent small birds for meat.

When enemies came to fight, God helped them to win.

God loved His people. But when they did not obey, He had to punish them.

One time God talked to Moses on a high mountain. God said how the people should live and worship Him. God told Moses how to make the tent for worship called the tabernacle. God gave Moses two pieces of stone where God wrote the Ten Commandments.

But while Moses was on the mountain, the people grew tired of waiting. They told Aaron, "Make us gods." So

Aaron made a golden calf. Then God punished the people. Many were killed.

Moses sent twelve spies to Canaan. When they came back, only two said, "God will help us." The other ten men said, "It is a good land, but strong giants live there. We are afraid." The people believed the ten men. They did not trust God. So God said all the people must stay in the wilderness a long, long time.

When some men told Moses, "God does not want you to be our leader," God made a great hole open in the ground. Those men and their families fell in and died.

Sometimes the people complained. When they said, "We are tired of this manna to eat," God sent snakes to bite the people. Many of them died.

For forty years the people traveled. God took good care of them all the time. He wanted them to trust Him.

Questions and Answers

1. Where did God's people travel?
   They traveled in the wilderness.

2. Did God's people always obey God?
   No, they did not always obey God.

3. How did God help His people?
   (Various answers are correct.)

Bible Verse to Learn

"Trust in the Lord, and do good." Psalm 37:3

16. Joshua Is the Leader

It was soon time for God's people to enter the land of Canaan. Moses told them to remember all God's laws and obey them. Then God would bless them. Moses said, "Remember all the good things God did for you."

Moses told them that Joshua would be the new leader. He told Joshua to be strong and to always obey God.

Moses had been a good leader, but one time when the people needed water, Moses had become angry. God had said, "Speak to the rock," but Moses hit it. So God told Moses he could not lead the people into Canaan.

Now it was time for Moses to die. But first God let him see beautiful Canaan from a high mountain. When Moses died, God buried him. No one saw his grave.

Joshua wanted to be a good leader. He helped the people get ready to enter Canaan. They had to cross the Jordan River. Joshua told the priests to go first. When the priests stepped into the water, God made the river stop flowing. All the people walked to the other side on dry ground.

They camped near a big city called Jericho. God told Joshua just what to do. Each day for six days, the people walked quietly around the big city. On the seventh day, they walked around the city seven times. Then they shouted, and God made the walls fall flat. They burned the city with fire.

God had said, "No one should keep anything for themselves." But one man disobeyed. Achan took some money and clothes from the city. He hid them under his tent.

Because Achan disobeyed, God did not help His people. Joshua asked God why there was trouble. God said, "Someone did not obey Me. He must be destroyed." God showed Joshua that it was Achan. The people stoned Achan and his family. Then God helped His people again.

All the days that Joshua was their leader, the children of Israel served the Lord. God blessed them.

Questions and Answers

1. Who was the leader after Moses died?
   Joshua was the new leader after Moses.

2. What happened at Jericho when the people shouted?
   The walls of the city fell flat.

3. Did God know Achan had disobeyed?
   Yes, God knew Achan had disobeyed.

Bible Verse to Learn
"We will serve the Lord." Joshua 24:15

17. Gideon Obeys God

After Joshua died, the people continued to serve the true God. But as the years went by, the children of Israel made friends with the people around them who worshiped idols. Sometimes they let their children marry persons who were not God's people. Then they worshiped idols too.

When God's people did evil and worshiped idols, God could not bless them. He let people from other lands come and make the children of Israel suffer. Then God's people would cry and pray to God.

God helped His people when they cried to Him. He gave them leaders called judges to save them from their enemies. God was with the judges and helped them.

One time the children of Israel had to hide in caves because the enemies would steal everything they could find. The people were very sad, but God heard their cry. God sent an angel to Gideon. He said, "Gideon, I will help you save My people." When Gideon gave food to the angel, the angel touched it with his staff, and fire burned it. Then the angel disappeared.

That night God told Gideon, "Tear down the altar to

the idol and build an altar for Me." Gideon obeyed.

God wanted Gideon to get an army ready to fight the enemies. But when the men came to Gideon, God said, "There are too many men. If the army is too big, they will not think they need to trust Me." So Gideon told all the men who were afraid to go home. Then God said, "There are still too many." So Gideon chose only the men who were careful to watch and be good soldiers.

The enemy had many, many people, but Gideon believed God would help him and his small army. Gideon put his men into three little groups. At night they went near the enemies. All at once they broke their pitchers and held up lamps. They blew their trumpets and shouted.

The enemies became so frightened that they started killing each other. God helped Gideon and his men so that those enemies did not make God's people suffer anymore.

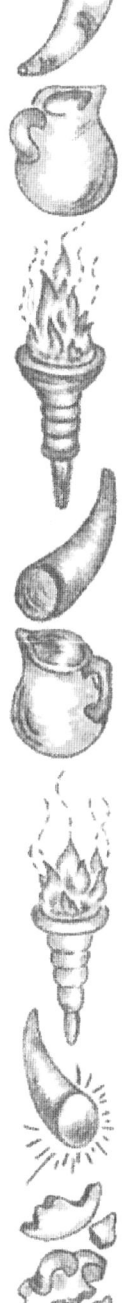

Questions and Answers

1. Did God want His people to worship idols?

   No, God wanted His people to worship Him.

2. Who wanted Gideon to get an army ready?

   God wanted Gideon to get an army ready.

3. When did Gideon and his men go near the army?

   Gideon and his men went at night.

Bible Verse to Learn

"Many times did he deliver them." Psalm 106:43

18. Samson Is Strong

One time when God's people did evil, God let the Philistines punish them. But God still loved His people. He sent an angel to speak to a woman and her husband. The angel said, "You will have a baby boy. You should never cut your son's hair because his long hair will be a sign that he belongs to God. He will begin to save Israel from the Philistines."

The man and his wife believed the angel. God gave them a baby boy named Samson. When Samson grew to be a man, he became a judge in Israel.

One time a lion came roaring at Samson. God helped him to be strong and to kill the lion with his hands.

Another time Samson caught three hundred foxes. He tied burning sticks to their tails. He let the foxes run in the Philistines' fields to punish the Philistines. The fire from the foxes' tails burned the crops in the fields.

One day Samson found a jawbone of a donkey. God helped him use it to kill one thousand Philistines. Then he threw the jawbone away. Later Samson became so thirsty that he thought he would die. God made water come out of the jawbone for Samson to drink.

Samson was in a Philistine city one night. The men waited near the city gate to catch him in the morning. But at midnight, Samson picked up the whole big city gate and its posts and carried them to the top of a hill in his own land. God helped him to be strong.

After this Samson loved a woman who tried to find out why he was so strong. Finally he told her that his hair had never been cut. While Samson slept, she told a man to cut off his hair. When Samson awoke, he was not strong anymore. He had disobeyed God. The Philistines took out his eyes and put him into prison.

Then the Philistines wanted to make fun of Samson. They brought him to a house full of people. Now his hair was growing long again. He stood at the middle pillars and prayed for God's help. Then he made the house fall down. Samson was strong when he obeyed God.

Questions and Answers

1. Did God want Samson to cut his hair?
   No, God wanted Samson to obey.

2. Did Samson use the jawbone of a fox or a donkey?
   Samson used the jawbone of a donkey.

3. When did Samson carry the big city gate away?
   Samson carried the gate away at midnight.

Bible Verse to Learn
"Be strong in the Lord." Ephesians 6:10

19. Ruth Loves Naomi

In the time when the judges ruled in Israel, there was a famine. The crops did not grow well. A certain man took his wife, Naomi, and two sons to live in another land where there was food.

While they were there, the man died. His two sons married wives named Ruth and Orpah. But after a few years, the two sons also died. This made Naomi very sad. She wanted to go back to her home in Bethlehem. She had heard that God had made the crops grow better, and now there was more food.

Orpah and Ruth wanted to be kind to Naomi and go with her. But Naomi said, "It is better for you to stay in your own land with your parents." So Orpah stayed with her family.

But Ruth loved Naomi very, very much. Ruth said, "Please let me go with you. I want to live where you live. Your people shall be my people. Your God shall be my God." So Naomi let Ruth go with her.

They came to Bethlehem when the people were just starting to gather barley in the fields. Ruth wanted to help Naomi. She asked, "May I pick up some grain in the fields?" Naomi said she could go.

Ruth came to a field belonging to a kind man named Boaz. Boaz saw Ruth. He asked who she was. His servant said, "She is the one who came back with Naomi. She is a good worker."

Boaz talked to Ruth. He said, "You may stay in my fields to work each day." Boaz also told his men to treat Ruth in a nice way. Boaz saw how kind Ruth was to Naomi. He helped Ruth and gave her food. Ruth was thankful. Now she could give more food to Naomi.

Boaz loved Ruth, and she became his wife. God gave them a baby boy named Obed. Naomi was happy to hold Ruth's little baby and to help care for him.

When Obed grew up, he had a son named Jesse. Jesse became the father of King David. God said, "The Saviour will be born from King David's family."

Questions and Answers

1. What made Naomi sad?

   Her husband and two sons died.

2. What kind of worker was Ruth?

   Ruth was a good worker.

3. Who became Boaz's wife?

   Ruth became Boaz's wife.

Bible Verse to Learn

"In God have I put my trust." Psalm 56:11

20. Samuel Helps Eli

Eli was the priest in Israel. He lived in the house of God at Shiloh. The people came there to worship.

One day Eli saw a woman praying. Her name was Hannah. She was very sad because she had no children. She promised that if God would give her a baby boy, then she would give him back to serve God all his life.

When Eli saw Hannah crying, he asked what was wrong. She said, "I have told all my trouble to God."

Eli said, "Go in peace. May God answer your prayer."

Hannah went home with her husband, and God did answer her prayer. He gave her a baby named Samuel.

Hannah kept her promise. When Samuel was old enough, his parents took him to Eli. Hannah said, "God answered my prayer. Now Samuel belongs to God." So Samuel stayed with Eli. Each year Hannah made a new coat and brought it to Samuel when she came to worship.

Eli was an old man, and Samuel was a good helper.

One night when Samuel lay down to sleep, he heard a voice call his name, "Samuel." He thought Eli called him, so he went to Eli. Samuel said, "Here am I."

But Eli said, "I did not call you. Go lie down."

Samuel went to lie down. Two more times, Samuel heard his name. Each time he went to Eli. But Eli had not called him. Then Eli said, "If you hear the voice again, say, 'Speak, Lord, for Thy servant heareth.' "

Samuel obeyed Eli. Then God talked to Samuel. God told Samuel that He would punish Eli and his sons because Eli did not stop his sons from doing bad things.

In the morning, Samuel got up and opened the doors of the house of God. When Eli asked Samuel what God said, Samuel told him everything that God had said.

Soon there was a war. Eli's two sons were killed. When Eli heard all the bad things that had happened, he fell off his seat, broke his neck, and died.

Samuel became the next judge in Israel. He helped the people worship God, and God was with him.

Questions and Answers

1. Did God answer Hannah's prayer?

   Yes, God gave her a baby boy.

2. Did Hannah keep her promise to God?

   Yes, Hannah took Samuel to stay at God's house.

3. Who called Samuel one night?

   God called Samuel one night.

Bible Verse to Learn

"Speak, Lord; for thy servant heareth." 1 Samuel 3:9

21. Saul Is the First King

When Samuel was getting older, his sons helped him rule Israel. But his sons were not always fair to the people.

The people said to Samuel, "We want a king to rule over us."

Samuel knew that God was leading His people. They did not need a king. So Samuel prayed.

God told Samuel, "The people may have a king, but tell them how it will be. The king will take their fields and animals and make the people be his servants." Samuel told the people what God had said. But the people wanted a king anyway.

One day a man's donkeys were lost. His son Saul hunted for them. But Saul could not find them. So he talked to Samuel. Samuel told him the donkeys were found. Samuel also told Saul, "God has chosen you to be the new king." Samuel poured oil on Saul's head to anoint him. Then Saul went home.

Soon Samuel called all the people together to tell them that Saul had been chosen to be king. The people wanted to see him, but Saul was hiding. When they found him, everyone shouted, "God save the king!" King Saul, the new king, was taller than any other man in Israel.

King Saul wanted to be a good king and help the people. At first he carefully obeyed what Samuel said.

Then one time there was trouble. Samuel told King Saul, "Wait until I come, and I will offer a sacrifice to God." But Saul became afraid. He did not wait long enough. Instead, he offered the sacrifice himself just before Samuel came.

Samuel was not pleased. He said, "God wants you to obey. Now God will not let your son be the next king. God will choose another man to be the next king. God will choose a man who loves to please God."

Saul was not sorry he disobeyed. He continued to take his own way when he thought he knew better than what Samuel said. Saul became sadder and sadder. He was a very sad man, and God did not bless him.

Questions and Answers

1. Who anointed the new king with oil?
   Samuel anointed the new king.

2. Did Saul always obey Samuel carefully?
   No, Saul did not always obey Samuel.

3. Would God let Saul's son be the next king?
   No, God would choose another man to be king.

Bible Verse to Learn

"Behold, to obey is better than sacrifice." 1 Samuel 15:22

22. David Is a Shepherd

God wanted Israel to have a king that would follow His ways. He said to Samuel, "Go to Bethlehem. Anoint one of Jesse's sons to be the next king." Jesse was the grandson of Boaz and Ruth.

So Samuel went to Bethlehem. He saw Jesse's eight sons. David was the youngest one. He took care of his father's sheep. God said that David was the one to be king some-day. Samuel anointed him with oil.

But David did not become king for a long time.

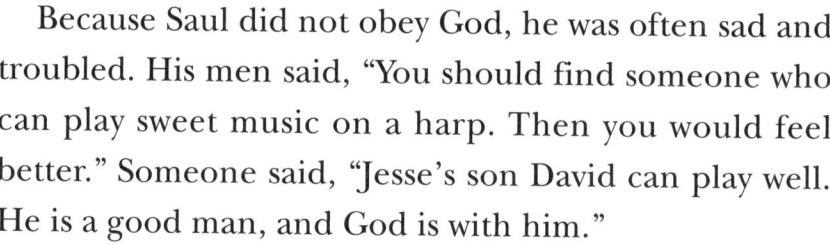

Because Saul did not obey God, he was often sad and troubled. His men said, "You should find someone who can play sweet music on a harp. Then you would feel better." Someone said, "Jesse's son David can play well. He is a good man, and God is with him."

Saul sent for David, and David played on his harp. This made Saul feel better. Then David went home.

The Philistines were enemies who worshiped idols. They came to fight Israel. They had a giant named Goliath. Each day he would shout, "Let a man come to me. If he kills me, we will be your servants. But if I kill him, you will serve us." Saul's army was afraid.

David's three oldest brothers were in Saul's army. One day David brought some food to his brothers. David heard what Goliath said. David said to Saul, "I will fight the giant. When I took care of the sheep, God helped me kill a lion and a bear. God will help me kill the giant too." Saul said David could go.

So David took five stones. He came near Goliath and said, "Everyone will know our God can save us." Then David put a stone in his sling. He killed the giant by God's help, and the Philistines ran away.

This made the people in Israel glad. But it made Saul angry because everyone liked David. Saul hated David so much he tried to kill him again and again.

Saul's son Jonathan loved David. They were good friends. David was very careful to do right and to be kind to Saul. God was with David.

Questions and Answers

1. Did Samuel anoint Jesse's oldest or youngest son?
   Samuel anointed Jesse's youngest son, David.

2. Who was sad and troubled when he disobeyed God?
   King Saul was sad and troubled.

3. Did the giant kill David?
   No, God helped David to kill the giant.

Bible Verse to Learn

"The Lord is my shepherd." Psalm 23:1

23. David Sits on the Throne

King Saul, the first king of Israel, had died in a battle. Jonathan and the other sons of Saul had died in the battle too.

Now David was the new king. He helped the people have courage to obey God. David wrote many songs for the people to sing to praise and worship God. David wanted to build a temple to worship God. But God said, "Your son will be the one to build My house." So David started to get things ready for his son to build God's house. David wanted to do as God had said.

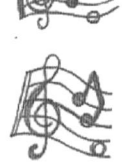

King David wanted to be kind to Jonathan's family because Jonathan had been a very good friend. David heard that Jonathan had a son Mephibosheth who had lame feet. So David sent for him. King David said, "I want you to live at my palace and eat here every day. I will give you the land that belonged to your family." Mephibosheth was thankful for the king's kindness.

Sometimes King David had troubles. One time while David was doing his work, his son Absalom was trying to be the next king. Absalom stood at the gate where people came to see the king. He talked friendly to the people. Soon many people agreed that he would be a good king instead of his father. David had to go away from the palace at Jerusalem to be safe. But David's friends were kind and helped him. When Absalom was killed in a woods, David came back to his throne again. God took care of David because he trusted God.

David was a good king, but sometimes when he was tempted, he did wrong. Then God punished him. One time he told his captain to count the people, but God was not pleased. God sent an angel to kill many people. King David was very sorry he had done wrong. The prophet told David to build an altar to God on a certain place where men threshed wheat. So David bought the threshing floor and did what the prophet said. Then God forgave David, and the punishment stopped.

As long as he lived, King David loved the Lord.

Questions and Answers

1. Did King David build the temple to God?
   No, God said David's son should build the temple.

2. Who was the lame son of Jonathan?
   Mephibosheth was the lame son.

3. Was David angry or sorry when he had done wrong?
   David was sorry he had done wrong.

Bible Verse to Learn
"I will be sorry for my sin." Psalm 38:18

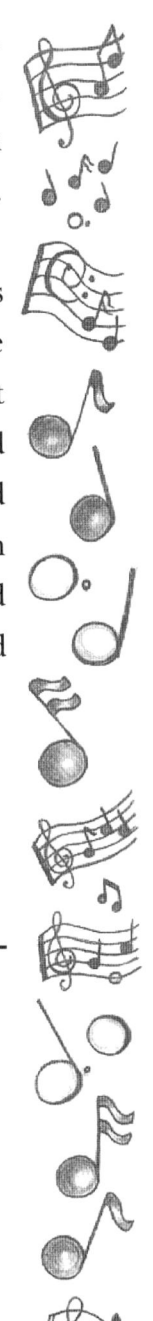

24. Solomon Builds the Temple

God told King David that his son Solomon would be the next king. Before King David died, he told Solomon that if he always obeyed God, God would help him.

King Solomon wanted to be a good king. He loved God and worshiped Him. One night God talked to Solomon. God asked, "What shall I give you?"

Solomon said, "I would like to be a wise king. I want to understand the best ways to help the people." God was pleased with Solomon's choice. God gave him great wisdom. God also gave him riches, honor, and long life.

King Solomon began to build God's house. Many people helped to build. They used big stones and fine cedar wood. They covered the whole house with gold. The temple was built very quietly. It took seven years to build it. At last the beautiful temple was finished.

Then King Solomon and all the people had a big feast to dedicate God's house. They killed many animals for sacrifices. Solomon prayed that God would dwell with His people and bless them. God was pleased. His glory filled the new temple with a cloud.

God helped King Solomon to do many wonderful things. Many people far away heard about his kingdom. The Queen of Sheba came to see if all the wonderful things were true. She brought rich gifts. She talked to Solomon and asked hard questions. When she heard his wise answers and saw all the wonderful things, she said, "I did not believe what I had heard. But now I can see that it is even so much more wonderful than they told me. Your people are happy, and God loves you, Solomon."

But King Solomon's people were not always happy. He did not always thank God for helping them. Solomon made the people work harder and harder to build more and more wonderful places. Also, Solomon loved many, many women. He started to worship idols because he wanted to please his wives. But God was not pleased. God could not bless Solomon when Solomon did evil.

Questions and Answers

1. Did Solomon choose to be wise or rich?

   Solomon chose to be wise.

2. What did they use to cover the whole temple?

   They covered the temple with gold.

3. Did Solomon always please God?

   No, Solomon did not always please God.

Bible Verse to Learn

"O worship the Lord." Psalm 96:9

61

25. Two Kings Start to Rule

God was not pleased when King Solomon did evil. God told the prophet, "I will choose another king besides Solomon's son. His son will rule only a small part of Israel. The other king will rule ten tribes of Israel."

After Solomon died, his son Rehoboam became king. The people said to Rehoboam, "Your father made life hard for us. Please make our lives easier now."

King Rehoboam said, "Go home, and come back in three days." Then Rehoboam asked other men for advice.

The old men said, "Listen to the people and be kind. Then the people will want to help you." The young men said, "Make life harder for the people."

In three days the people came back. King Rehoboam listened to the young men. He told the people, "I will make life harder for you than my father did."

The people were sad. Ten tribes of Israel said, "We will not let Rehoboam be our king. We will go home."

God chose Jeroboam to be the new king for the ten unhappy tribes. Only two tribes stayed and worked for King Rehoboam. King Rehoboam lived at Jerusalem.

Now King Jeroboam's people did not have a temple to worship God. King Jeroboam was afraid to let his people go to the temple King Solomon built at Jerusalem. So King Jeroboam did a very bad thing. He made two golden calves for his people to worship in their own land.

God was not pleased. He sent a prophet to warn the king. King Jeroboam was standing near the one golden calf. The prophet cried, "A new king named Josiah will get rid of this ungodly idol worship."

King Jeroboam tried to grab the prophet, but his hand became stiff and would not move. Also God made the idol's altar fall apart. The king said, "Please pray for me." So the prophet prayed, and God healed the king's hand. But Jeroboam did not listen to God's warning. He and the people continued to worship idols. God was not pleased. So God punished King Jeroboam.

Questions and Answers

1. Which men did King Rehoboam listen to?
   King Rehoboam listened to the young men.

2. Did all the people stay with King Rehoboam?
   No, only two tribes stayed with him.

3. What bad thing did King Jeroboam do?
   He made two golden calves to worship.

Bible Verse to Learn

"Depart from evil, and do good." Psalm 34:14

26. God Helps Elijah

Even though God punished King Jeroboam and his family, the kings that ruled after Jeroboam kept right on worshiping idols.

One king named Ahab was very wicked. God told the good prophet Elijah to talk to King Ahab. Elijah said, "Because you do not worship God, God will not send rain until I say He will."

Then God told Elijah to hide by a brook so Ahab could not find

him. God sent ravens to give food to Elijah every morning and every evening. Elijah drank water from the brook until the brook dried up because there was no rain.

God told Elijah where to go. Elijah went to that village and asked a widow for food. She only had a little for herself and her son, but she shared it with Elijah. God made her food last until God sent rain.

When the widow's son was so sick that he died, Elijah prayed, and God made her son alive again. Then she said, "Now I know you are a man of God."

After three and one-half years of no rain, God told Elijah to talk to King Ahab again. Elijah said, "Tell all the people to go to Mount Carmel."

King Ahab obeyed. On Mount Carmel, Elijah said, "We will see who is the true God. You offer an animal to the idol, Baal, and I will offer an animal to the Lord. The one who sends fire on the altar is the true God."

So the prophets of Baal put a young bull on their altar. All day long they cried loudly and hurt themselves. But their idol could not hear, or see, or send fire.

In the evening, Elijah said, "Come near to me." He used twelve stones to build God's altar. He put on wood and a young bull. He said, "Pour water on it." So they poured twelve barrels of water on it. Then Elijah prayed. Right away fire from God in heaven burned the bull, the wood, the stones, the dust, and the water.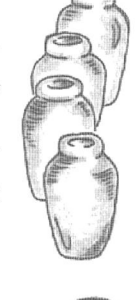

All the people said, "The Lord, He is the God!"

Elijah said, "Kill all the prophets of Baal." God did not want the people to worship idols.

Questions and Answers

1. Did King Ahab worship God or the idol?

   King Ahab worshiped the idol.

2. What brought food to Elijah at the brook?

   The ravens brought food to Elijah.

3. Did the idol or God send fire?

   God in heaven sent fire.

Bible Verse to Learn

"The Lord, he is the God." 1 Kings 18:39

27. God Punishes King Ahab

After the prophets of Baal were killed, God sent a very great rain. This should have made everyone thankful to God.

But Jezebel, King Ahab's wicked wife, was not thankful. When she heard that the false prophets were dead, she was very angry. Jezebel said, "Elijah must die."

Now Elijah had to run and hide. He went alone into the wilderness. He was so sad that he asked God to let him die.

But God wanted Elijah to do more work for Him. God said, "There are many people in Israel who have never worshiped Baal." This made Elijah feel better. God also told him to choose a young man named Elisha to help him and to be the next prophet.

A prophet was a man who told the king and the people what God said. Many times the prophets had to warn people, like King Ahab, who were doing wrong.

One time King Ahab saw a vineyard near his palace that he liked very much. He wanted to buy it. He talked to the owner named Naboth.

Naboth said, "I cannot sell this vineyard to you because

it has belonged to our family for many years."

This made King Ahab very displeased. He was so unhappy that he went home and would not even eat.

Jezebel asked, "What is wrong, Ahab?" He told her that he could not have the vineyard he wanted.

Then Jezebel did something very bad. She wrote letters to the rulers in Naboth's city. She wanted men to tell lies about Naboth so that he would be stoned. The rulers did as her letters said. When Ahab heard that Naboth was dead, he went to take the vineyard.

But God knew what had happened. God sent Elijah to meet King Ahab. King Ahab did not like to see Elijah. He called the prophet his enemy. Elijah said, "Because you have done evil, God says you and Jezebel must die."

King Ahab was killed in battle, and Jezebel was thrown out of a window. What God said came true.

Questions and Answers

1. What kind of woman was Jezebel?

   Jezebel was a very wicked woman.

2. Why did Elijah have to run and hide?

   Jezebel said he must die.

3. Was Elijah or Naboth stoned?

   Naboth was stoned.

Bible Verse to Learn

"The Lord is against them that do evil." 1 Peter 3:12

28. Elijah Goes to Heaven

After Elisha was chosen to be a prophet, he became Elijah's helper. One day when they were at a place called Gilgal, Elijah said to Elisha, "Stay here while I go on to Bethel."

But Elisha would not leave him. So they went on together.

At Bethel some young prophets said to Elisha, "Do you know that the Lord is going to take your master away from you today?"

"Yes," said Elisha, "I know it."

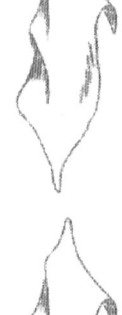

Then Elijah said that Elisha should stay at Bethel and he would go on to Jericho. But Elisha said, "No, I will not leave you." So they both went to Jericho.

The young prophets at Jericho also asked Elisha if he knew that God would take away his master that day. Elisha again said, "Yes, I know it."

Once more Elijah asked Elisha to stay while he went on, but Elisha would not leave him. Together they came to the Jordan. There Elijah hit the Jordan River with his mantle. God parted the waters. The two prophets walked across on a dry path to the other side.

Now Elijah asked Elisha a question. "What shall I do for you before I am taken away?"

Elisha answered, "Please let me have a double portion of your spirit."

Elijah knew that only God could give that. But he promised, "If you see me when I am taken to heaven, you will have what you asked."

They continued to walk and talk together. Suddenly a chariot and horses of fire appeared and separated them. Elisha watched Elijah go up to heaven in a whirlwind.

Elisha cried, "My father, my father!" Soon he could not see Elijah anymore.

Elisha picked up Elijah's mantle that had fallen. He walked back to the Jordan River. He hit the water with the mantle, and he walked across on dry ground. He had so much to remember. He had a great God to serve.

When the young prophets met him, they saw that the spirit of Elijah was with Elisha.

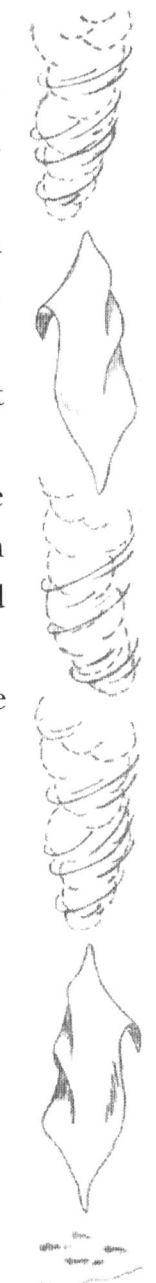

Questions and Answers

1. Did Elisha want to leave Elijah?
   No, Elisha wanted to go with Elijah.

2. Did Elisha know Elijah would be taken away?
   Yes, Elisha knew God would take Elijah.

3. How did Elijah go to heaven?
   Elijah went to heaven in a whirlwind.

Bible Verse to Learn

"Elijah went up by a whirlwind into heaven." 2 Kings 2:11

29. Elisha Helps Others

Elisha was a prophet of God. When people had trouble, they often asked Elisha what to do.

One time some men told Elisha their water was not good. Elisha threw salt into their spring, and God made the water good to drink and good to water the ground.

When the king wanted to know how to fight the enemy, Elisha told them just what God said. Then God's people won the battle.

A certain widow had two sons. A man was going to take her boys away if she could not pay him money. She had some oil, so Elisha told her what to do. She borrowed many, many vessels from her neighbors. Then she shut the door and poured oil into each vessel. God made the oil be enough to fill all the vessels. She sold the oil and paid the money. She even had money left.

God helped her when she obeyed Elisha.

Another woman often gave Elisha food to eat. She and her husband made a room where Elisha could rest when he came to their town. They put a bed, a table, a stool, and a candle in his room. They were kind to the good prophet, so God gave them a son. When the child became

sick and died, they told Elisha. Elisha prayed, and God
made the boy alive again.

When there was not much food in the land, the food
they did have to eat at one place was bad. Elisha threw
some flour into the food, and God made it good to eat.

In another country lived a man named Naaman who
had leprosy. His wife's maid told him about the prophet
of God. So Naaman came to Elisha. Elisha said he should
wash in the Jordan River seven times. When Naaman
obeyed, he was healed. He wanted to give gifts to the
prophet, but Elisha would not take any gifts. Elisha knew
that God had taken Naaman's leprosy away.

Elisha made an iron ax head swim when it accidentally
fell into the river. He helped the people many other times
too. Elisha did wonderful things because God was with
him. He loved and served God all his life.

Questions and Answers

1. What wonderful things did Elisha do?
   (Various answers are correct.)

2. Did the man take the widow's two boys?
   No, God helped her to pay the money.

3. What river did Naaman wash in?
   Naaman washed in the Jordan River.

Bible Verse to Learn

"Give glory to the Lord your God." Jeremiah 13:16

30. Jonah Is Called to Preach

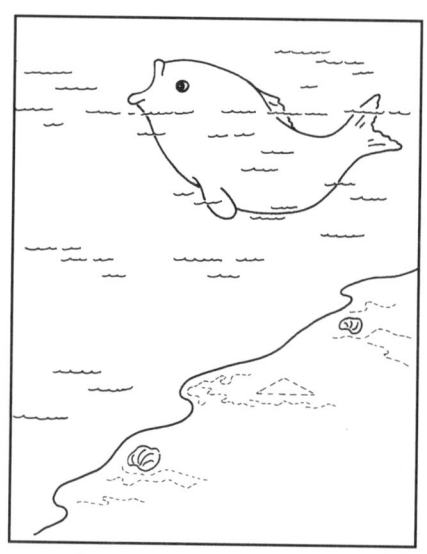

Jonah was a prophet of God soon after Elisha died. Jonah spoke what God said.

But when God told Jonah to go and preach to Nineveh, Jonah did not want to obey. Nineveh was a big city in the enemy's land. Sometimes those enemies would fight against Israel. Nineveh was a very wicked city where the people worshiped idols. Jonah did not want to preach to them.

So Jonah tried to run away from God. But no one can run away from God. God can see us everywhere we go.

Jonah went to Joppa and got on a ship. He went down into the ship and fell asleep. Out on the water, away from the land, God sent a great storm. The sailors were greatly afraid. They threw things out of the ship to make it more safe. They cried to their gods. But their gods could not help them. The captain woke Jonah and said, "Cry to your God."

Jonah knew he was not obeying God. He told the men, "I worship the God in heaven, who made the sea and the land." Jonah also said he was running away from God.

This made the sailors even more afraid. "What shall we

do so that the storm will stop?" they asked.

Jonah told them to throw him into the water and then the sea would be calm again. The men did not want Jonah to drown. They tried to row to land, but they could not. So they threw Jonah into the water as he said. Then the storm stopped, and they worshiped God in heaven.

Jonah did not drown because God sent a big fish to swallow him. Jonah was inside the fish for three days. Now he was sorry. He prayed and promised to obey God. God told the fish to vomit Jonah out on the shore.

Then Jonah did what God said. He went to Nineveh. He preached God's message. The king and all the people listened to him. They cried to God and stopped doing evil things. God forgave them. He did not punish them at that time. Jonah learned that God loves all people and wants everyone to do what is right.

Questions and Answers

1. What kind of city was Nineveh?
   Nineveh was a very wicked city.

2. Could the sailors' gods help them?
   No, their gods could not help them.

3. Why didn't Jonah drown in the water?
   God sent a big fish to swallow him.

Bible Verse to Learn
"Thou God seest me." Genesis 16:13

31. Two Good Kings Trust God

God's people had good kings and bad kings. King Hezekiah was a good king. He broke down the idols that the bad kings had made. He wanted all the people to trust God and to obey God's laws.

When the enemy tried to make trouble, King Hezekiah tried to make peace and not fight. But the enemy came to fight anyway. So King Hezekiah told all the people to keep quiet and trust God.

One captain of the enemy's army loudly told the people not to believe that God could save them. The people obeyed King Hezekiah and did not say a word.

When King Hezekiah heard this, he prayed. God sent the good prophet Isaiah to tell the king not to be afraid. God made the enemy hear about trouble in their own land, so the enemy's army went home.

Then the enemy sent a letter to say they would come back again. King Hezekiah took the letter to the temple and spread it before the Lord. Again Isaiah brought God's message to the king. That night God's angel killed many people in the enemy's camp. The rest of the army went home. God saved His people who trusted Him.

After King Hezekiah died, there were two bad kings who worshiped idols. The next king was Josiah. He began to reign when he was eight years old. He was the good king that the prophet told King Jeroboam about years before when King Jeroboam made the two golden calves. What God said came true. King Josiah got rid of the idols in the land, and he repaired God's house.

Many workers helped to make the temple a beautiful place to worship God again. While they cleaned the rooms, they found a lost book. It was God's Law that the bad kings had forgotten. A man read it to the king. The king wanted to obey what God said. So the king sent for all the people to come and hear God's Law.

Now the people helped the king destroy more idols. They kept the Passover feast as God commanded. King Josiah wanted to obey God's Law all the time.

Questions and Answers

1. Did King Hezekiah trust God or the idols?
   King Hezekiah trusted God.

2. Where did King Hezekiah take the enemy's letter?
   He took it to the temple.

3. What did the workers find in the temple?
   They found the lost Book that was God's Law.

Bible Verse to Learn

"I will trust, and not be afraid." Isaiah 12:2

32. Jeremiah Speaks God's Words

God wanted His people to obey Him. He sent many prophets to warn them when they did wrong.

Jeremiah was a faithful prophet. He often cried because the people worshiped idols. God had chosen Jeremiah to be a prophet before he was born. God helped him when the people did not want to hear the truth. God told Jeremiah not to be afraid. God promised to be with him and to keep him safe.

God saw all the idol worship. God said He would punish Israel for their sin. God would let the enemy come and take Israel far away from Canaan. God's people would have to live in the enemy's land seventy years.

God wanted these words written in a book. Jeremiah spoke God's words to his friend Baruch, and Baruch wrote all the words in a scroll.

Then Baruch went to the temple and read the words to all the people. When the king's men heard about it, they wanted Baruch to read it to them too. Then they told Baruch, "You and Jeremiah hide so no one can find you."

A man read the words to the king. King Jehoiakim did not fear God. He took a knife and cut off the pages after they were read. He threw them into the fire. Soon the whole roll was burned. Some of the men did not want it burned, but the king did not care. He was not sorry for doing evil. He wanted to punish Jeremiah and Baruch, but the Lord hid them.

God told Jeremiah, "Write all the words again and more words too. The terrible things will surely happen."

Soon another man became king. King Zedekiah did not want to hear God's warning either. Some of the king's men said Jeremiah was trying to help the enemy. So they put him into a deep hole. Jeremiah sank into the mud.

Some kind men helped Jeremiah. One man said, "Put these old rags under your arms so the ropes will not hurt you." Then they pulled Jeremiah up out of the hole.

God was with Jeremiah as He promised. All God's words came true. God wanted His people to worship Him.

Questions and Answers

1. Who wrote God's words in a scroll?

   Baruch wrote the words in a scroll.

2. Who burned the words of the scroll?

   King Jehoiakim burned the scroll.

3. Did the words of God come true?

   Yes, God's words came true.

Bible Verse to Learn

"Every word of God is pure." Proverbs 30:5

33. Four Friends Remember God

The enemy came to Israel just as God had said. They took many of God's people far away to a strange land. The enemy broke down the wall of Jerusalem and burned the houses. The king's palace and the beautiful temple were burned. God was punishing His people.

In the faraway land, the king said, "Choose the best young men from Jerusalem to help in my palace. Teach them my language and give them my food."

Daniel, Shadrach, Meshach, Abednego, and other young men were chosen. Daniel and his three friends wanted to obey God. God's Law said they should not eat some of the king's food. So they asked their master for other food. The master was afraid to disobey the king, but he agreed to try it for ten days. After ten days these four friends looked healthier than the other men. So they did not have to eat the king's food.

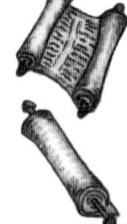

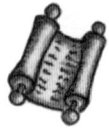

At the end of three years, the king wanted to test all the young men. He found that these four friends were ten times better than all his own wise men.

One night the king dreamed, but he forgot his dream.

He wanted to remember, but no one could tell him. He became so angry he said, "All the wise men must die." When Daniel and his friends heard about it, they prayed. God told Daniel the dream and what it meant. So Daniel told the king, and all the wise men were saved.

Then the king made a big, tall idol. He said, "Tell everyone to bow down when they hear the music." But Shadrach, Meshach, and Abednego did not bow down. They wanted to obey God. This made the king very angry. He said they must be thrown into a very hot furnace. The fire was so hot, it killed the men who threw them in. But God did not let the three faithful men burn. The three men walked out of the fire without being hurt. Then the king knew their God was great.

God blessed these young men because they remembered to obey God even in a strange land.

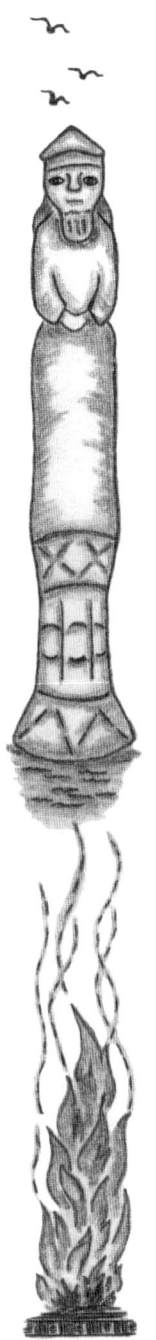

Questions and Answers

1. Did the four friends become wise or weak?

   They became wiser than the other men.

2. What did the king forget?

   The king forgot his dream.

3. Did the faithful men burn in the fire?

   No, God did not let them burn.

Bible Verse to Learn

"We will remember the name of the Lord." Psalm 20:7

34. Daniel Prays to God

God's people were living in the strange land far from Canaan. A new king saw that Daniel was wise and good. He was kind to others. So this king made Daniel his best helper to rule the land.

But some other men did not like Daniel to rule them. They watched Daniel to see if he did anything wrong. They wanted to tell the king so Daniel would have trouble.

But Daniel was always careful to do what was right. The men tried to think of another way to make trouble for Daniel. They knew that Daniel was faithful to pray to God every day. So they came to the king and said, "O King, live forever. We want you to make a new law. Tell everyone to pray only to you for thirty days. If they pray to anyone else, they should be thrown to the hungry lions."

So the king made the law. Then those men kept watching Daniel. They saw that he still went to his room and prayed to the true God three times each day.

They hurried to tell the king. "O King, Daniel does not obey your new law. He must be thrown to the lions."

When the king heard this, he was sorry he had made

the foolish law. He tried and tried to think of a way to save Daniel. Finally in the evening, he had to tell his helpers to throw Daniel into the den of lions. That night the king could not sleep at all.

Early in the morning, the king went quickly to the den of lions. He called sadly, "Daniel, Daniel, did your God keep you safe?"

Daniel had been with the fierce lions all night. He answered, "O King, God sent His angel and shut the lions' mouths. The lions have not hurt me."

How glad the king was! He told the men to take Daniel up out of the den. Then they threw the people in who had found fault with Daniel. Right away the lions killed them and broke all their bones.

The king said, "Everyone should fear the God who saved Daniel. He is the true God."

Questions and Answers

1. What did Daniel do three times each day?

    Daniel prayed to God three times each day.

2. Did the king want the lions to hurt Daniel?

    No, the king tried to save Daniel.

3. Why didn't the lions hurt Daniel?

    God sent His angel to shut the lions' mouths.

Bible Verse to Learn

"My God hath sent his angel." Daniel 6:22

35. Queen Esther Saves Her People

God's people were still living in the strange land. God's people were called Jews.

One time the king of the land had a great feast. During the feast, the queen did something that displeased the king. The king asked his wise men what to do. They said, "The queen did wrong. Do not let her be queen anymore. You must choose a new queen."

The king wanted many young women to come to his palace. He was going to choose a new queen. A beautiful woman named Esther came with the others. She was a Jew. Her father and mother had died. Her older cousin Mordecai took care of her as his own daughter.

When the king saw the lovely women one at a time, he loved Esther best of all. He put the crown on her head. Now Esther was the new queen.

Every day Mordecai the Jew stayed near the king's palace. He wanted to hear how Queen Esther was.

A proud man named Haman worked for the king. The king said everyone should bow to Haman. But Mordecai would not bow to Haman. This made Haman angry.

Haman said to the king, "The Jews in your land do not obey you. Make a law that they should be killed."

The king said Haman could make the law. But the king did not know Queen Esther was a Jew.

All the Jews cried when they heard the new law. Mordecai sent a message to Queen Esther. He said Queen Esther should ask the king to save her people. Queen Esther was afraid to go to the king. But she wanted to obey Mordecai. She asked all the Jews to pray to God.

Then Queen Esther went to the king. She asked him to save her people. The king listened to Queen Esther. He made a new law to save the Jews.

Now the Jews did not need to die. The king made Mordecai a great man. Proud Haman was killed.

The Jews were very, very glad that God had heard their prayer. God had helped Queen Esther to be brave.

Questions and Answers

1. Who did the king choose to be the new queen?
   The king chose Esther to be the new queen.

2. Why were the Jews so sad?
   The new law said they must be killed.

3. Was Mordecai or Haman killed?
   Haman was killed.

Bible Verse to Learn

"The Jews had joy and gladness." Esther 8:17

36. God's People Go Home

It was time for God's people to go back to their own land. They had stayed in the strange land for seventy years as God had said. Now God made the king willing to let the Jews go home.

One group went first. They started to build the temple. The people were so happy, they praised God. But soon some enemies made them stop.

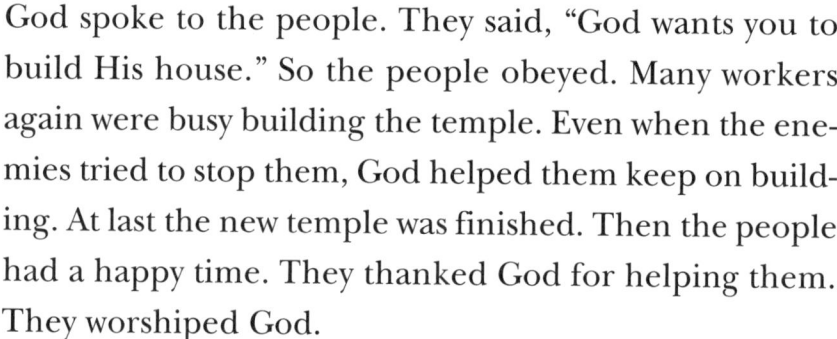

After a time, two prophets of God spoke to the people. They said, "God wants you to build His house." So the people obeyed. Many workers again were busy building the temple. Even when the enemies tried to stop them, God helped them keep on building. At last the new temple was finished. Then the people had a happy time. They thanked God for helping them. They worshiped God.

After this another group came back to their own land. Ezra was the leader this time. Ezra studied God's Law. He wanted to obey God's Law and teach it to the people. Ezra prayed and trusted God to help the group come safely home. God kept them safe from the enemies.

When Ezra got back to Jerusalem, he saw the new

temple. But he also saw that the people were not obeying God's Law. He wanted to teach the people, but it was a very rainy time.

A man named Nehemiah still worked in the king's palace far away. When he heard about the troubles at Jerusalem, he cried and prayed. The king said Nehemiah could go and help his people. So Nehemiah led another group of people back to Jerusalem.

There Nehemiah helped the people build the big city walls. The enemies made fun of them. Also the enemies became angry and tried to fight. But God helped His people keep on building. They worked and watched and prayed. Finally the big walls were finished.

Then all the people came to hear Ezra read God's Law. They listened quietly. They wanted to do what God said. God's people were happy and thankful.

Questions and Answers

1. Did God want them to build the temple?
   Yes, God wanted them to build the temple.

2. Who helped the people build the big city walls?
   Nehemiah helped the people build the walls.

3. What did Ezra read to the people?
   Ezra read God's Law to the people.

Bible Verse to Learn

"The people had a mind to work." Nehemiah 4:6

"And that from a child thou hast known the holy scriptures."   *2 Timothy 3:15*

"All scripture is given by inspiration of God."   *2 Timothy 3:16*

"For the word of God is quick, and powerful."   *Hebrews 4:12*

"Blessed is he that keepeth the sayings . . . of this book."   *Revelation 22:7*

New

Testament

37. Two Special Babies

Zacharias was a priest. He and his wife Elisabeth had no children. But they were faithful to God. One day an angel appeared to Zacharias in the temple. The angel said, "Zacharias, God will give you a son. You shall call his name John. He will do special work for God."

Zacharias did not believe the angel because he and his wife were very old. So the angel said, "Because you did not believe my words, you

will not be able to speak until your son is born." Now Zacharias could not say a word.

God kept His promise. A baby boy was born in the home of Zacharias and Elisabeth. When the friends wondered what the father would call the baby, Zacharias

wrote, "His name is John." Immediately Zacharias could speak. He praised God. The people were surprised. They said, "This child shall be a special person."

About this time, God sent an angel to a virgin named Mary. The angel said, "God has chosen you to be the mother of Jesus. Jesus is the Son of God." How happy Mary was! She wanted to please God.

Mary lived in Nazareth. Then the king wanted everyone

to be taxed. So Joseph and Mary had to go to Bethlehem. Many other people were going to Bethlehem too.

When Joseph and Mary came to Bethlehem, it was time for Baby Jesus to be born. But there was no room for them in the inn. So when Jesus was born, Mary laid her dear little baby in a manger.

Out in the fields, the shepherds were watching their sheep. The sky was dark. Suddenly an angel appeared. The sky became very bright. The angel announced, "Fear not; I have good news. A Saviour is born in Bethlehem." Soon many angels appeared. They praised God.

After the angels went back to heaven, the shepherds went to Bethlehem. They found Baby Jesus in the manger.

The shepherds told many people the wonderful news that Jesus the Saviour had come into the world.

Questions and Answers

1. Who told Zacharias he would have a son?

    An angel told Zacharias he would have a son.

2. Where was Baby Jesus born?

    Baby Jesus was born in Bethlehem.

3. Who came to see Baby Jesus in the manger?

    The shepherds came to see Baby Jesus.

Bible Verse to Learn

"God . . . loved us, and sent his Son." 1 John 4:10

38. A Bright Star Shines

When Jesus was a small baby, His parents took Him to the temple. A man named Simeon was there. God's Spirit told him that he would not die until he had seen the Saviour. Simeon held Baby Jesus in his arms. He blessed God. Simeon was happy.

An aged woman named Anna came into the temple. She saw Baby Jesus too. She told many people that the Saviour was born.

About the time Jesus was born, a bright star shone in the sky. Some wise men from far away followed the star. They came to Jerusalem. They asked King Herod, "Where is the King of the Jews born? We have seen His star in the East. We have come to worship Him."

This made King Herod afraid. He asked some teachers of the Jews where Jesus was to be born. They said, "In Bethlehem, the Scriptures tell us."

King Herod told the wise men, "Go to Bethlehem and find the child. Then come back and tell me. I want to worship Him too." This was not true. Herod wanted to kill Jesus so that Jesus could not be the king.

The wise men went to Bethlehem. The star showed

them the house where Jesus was. They were very happy
to see and worship Jesus. They gave gold and other rich
gifts to Jesus. Then God told the wise men in a dream,
"Do not go back to King Herod." So they went home
another way.

When the wise men left, an angel told Joseph in a
dream, "Herod will try to kill Jesus. You must take Mary
and the child far away into Egypt. Stay there until I tell
you it is safe to come back." Joseph obeyed. He took Mary
and Jesus at night to go to Egypt.

Soon King Herod sent men to kill all the babies near
Bethlehem. How the mothers cried for their babies! But
Jesus was safe with His parents far away in Egypt.

After King Herod died, God told Joseph to come back
to the land of Israel. Joseph and Mary and Jesus came
back and lived in Nazareth.

Questions and Answers

1. How did the wise men know Jesus was born?
   They saw His star in the sky.

2. Did King Herod want to worship Jesus?
   No, he wanted to kill Jesus.

3. What did the wise men give to Jesus?
   They gave gold and other rich gifts.

Bible Verse to Learn
"God . . . knoweth all things." 1 John 3:20

39. Jesus Goes to the Temple

Jesus lived with His family at Nazareth. Joseph was a carpenter. Jesus helped Joseph and Mary and obeyed them.

On Sabbath days they went to the synagogue. They listened as the Scriptures were read. Once a year, Joseph and Mary went to the temple in Jerusalem.

When Jesus was twelve years old, He went along with His parents to the temple in Jerusalem.

Many friends and relatives went too. The families walked and talked together.

After staying in Jerusalem several days, the group started home. Mary and Joseph thought Jesus was with their friends. They traveled one whole day. Then Jesus' parents looked for Jesus. But they could not find Him anywhere in the whole group. How sad they were! "Where could Jesus be?" they wondered.

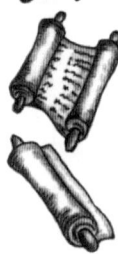

Jesus' parents went back to Jerusalem. They kept looking for Jesus. After three days, they found Him in the temple, talking with the teachers of the Jews. Jesus listened to the teachers. Jesus also asked questions. The teachers were surprised that Jesus understood so many things about the Scriptures.

When His parents found Him, His mother asked, "Why didn't You come with us? We didn't know where You were. We have been looking for You."

Jesus answered, "Why were you looking for Me? Didn't you know that I should be here doing what My heavenly Father wants Me to do?"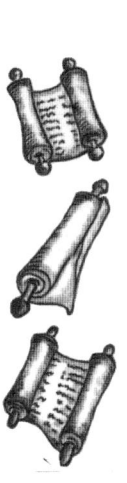

Jesus' parents did not understand all that Jesus was talking about. But they wanted to take care of their son. So Jesus went back home to Nazareth with them.

Joseph and Mary had other children younger than Jesus. The boys were James and Joses and Simon and Judas. Jesus was kind to His brothers and sisters.

Jesus kept growing taller and wiser. He loved others, and many people loved Him. Jesus always did what pleased God, His heavenly Father.

Questions and Answers

1. Did Jesus live in Nazareth or Jerusalem?
   Jesus lived in Nazareth.

2. Where did Jesus go when He was twelve years old?
   Jesus went to the temple in Jerusalem.

3. Who looked for Jesus for three days?
   Jesus' parents looked for Him for three days.

Bible Verse to Learn
"Jesus increased in wisdom and stature." Luke 2:52

40. John and Jesus Obey God

When John grew up, he did special work for God. John preached that everyone should be sorry for their sins and stop doing wrong.

John told the people, "Jesus is coming soon." John wanted the people to be ready to hear and follow Jesus. John baptized people in the Jordan River.

One day Jesus came to John. Jesus wanted to please God, so He asked John to baptize Him. John

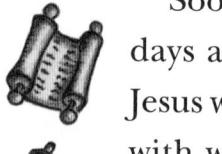

baptized Jesus in the Jordan River. When they came up out of the water, God's Spirit came down from heaven like a dove and sat upon Jesus. Also a voice from heaven said, "This is my beloved Son, in whom I am well pleased."

Soon after this, Jesus stayed in the wilderness for forty days and forty nights. Satan tempted Jesus to sin. But Jesus would not do what Satan said. Jesus answered Satan with words from the Scriptures. God was pleased that Jesus did not obey Satan. God sent angels to comfort and help Jesus.

One day Jesus and his mother went to a wedding. Many other friends were there too. They had good food to eat and wine to drink. It was a happy time.

But after a while, all the wine was gone. Jesus' mother knew their friends had no more wine. She told Jesus, "They have no wine."

Jesus' mother also told the servants, "Whatever Jesus tells you, you should do."

Six big waterpots were sitting nearby. Jesus said, "Fill the waterpots with water."

The servants filled them to the top with water.

Jesus said, "Now take some to your master."

When the master tasted it, he said, "This is the best wine we have had. The best wine should have been given to the people first of all."

Jesus had done a wonderful thing! He had turned water into wine. It was His first miracle. His friends believed that He is the Son of God.

Questions and Answers

1. Where did John baptize the people?

   John baptized the people in the Jordan River.

2. Did Jesus do what Satan told Him to do?

   No, Jesus would not do what Satan said.

3. What was the first miracle Jesus did?

   Jesus turned water into wine.

Bible Verse to Learn

"This is my beloved Son." Matthew 3:17

41. Jesus Chooses His Disciples

Jesus wanted people to learn the good news from God. God loves everyone. God wants everyone to believe and obey Him. God sent Jesus, His Son, to save people from their sins.

One day Jesus sat in Peter's boat near the shore and taught the people. The people were on the land close to the lake. When Jesus was finished teaching, He said to Peter, "Take your boat out to the deep water. Let your net down to catch fish."

Peter answered, "We fished all night and didn't catch any fish. But because You say so, I will do it."

Soon the net was so full they needed some fishermen in another boat to help them. The other fishermen were brothers named James and John.

Peter was surprised and afraid. But Jesus said, "Do not be afraid. From now on you will fish for men." Jesus wanted Peter and his friends to bring men to God to be saved.

When the two boats came to the land, the fishermen left their work and followed Jesus. They wanted to learn more from their wonderful Friend.

Another day Jesus saw Matthew sitting at his work. People paid tax money to Matthew. Jesus said to him, "Follow Me." Matthew stood up and followed Jesus.

Jesus had many friends. But Jesus wanted to choose certain friends to be His helpers. So Jesus went out into a mountain to pray. He prayed to God all night.

The next day Jesus chose twelve men to be His helpers. He chose the four fishermen: Peter, Andrew, James, and John. He chose Matthew, the tax collector. He chose Philip, who lived in the same town as Peter and his brother Andrew. The other helpers were Philip's friend Bartholomew, Thomas, another James, Judas, Simon, and Judas Iscariot.

These twelve helpers were called Jesus' twelve disciples. They often went with Jesus when Jesus was teaching and healing the people.

Questions and Answers

1. What did the fishermen catch in their net?

   The fishermen caught many fish.

2. What did people pay to Matthew?

   The people paid tax money to Matthew.

3. How many disciples did Jesus choose?

   Jesus chose twelve disciples.

Bible Verse to Learn

"Ever follow that which is good." 1 Thessalonians 5:15

42. Friends Help a Sick Man

Many people heard about the wonderful things Jesus did and the words He taught.

One time Peter's wife's mother had a fever. So Jesus healed her. That evening, many people came to Jesus. They brought other sick people, and Jesus healed them.

The next morning, Jesus rose up early. He went away alone to pray to God in a quiet place.

When Peter and his friends found Jesus, they walked together to other towns. Jesus preached in the synagogues. He healed many people because He loved the people. He wanted to help them.

In one town, Jesus went into a house. Many people came to hear Him. The house was full. Still many more people stood outside. Jesus preached to the people.

That day four friends brought a sick man on a bed to Jesus. But they could not get near Jesus. So they did a strange thing. They took the sick man up on the roof. They made a hole in the roof. They let the man on the bed down, down, down to where Jesus was.

When Jesus saw what happened, He knew the friends believed He could heal the sick man. But Jesus wanted people to know that He could forgive sins too. So Jesus said to the man, "I forgive all your sins."

Some of the leaders of the Jews were in the house. They did not like what Jesus said. They thought, "Why does Jesus say He forgives sins? Only God can forgive sins."

Jesus knew what these men thought. He said, "I want you to know that I have God's power. I can forgive sins just as well as I can heal this man."

Then Jesus said to the sick man, "Get up and carry your bed to your house."

Right away the happy man took up his bed and walked home. How surprised the people were! They said, "We never saw anything so wonderful!" They were sure that Jesus is the Saviour of the world. They thanked God for sending Jesus to help all people.

Questions and Answers

1. How did the sick man get into the full house?

   He was let down through a hole in the roof.

2. Did Jesus heal the sick man?

   Yes, Jesus healed the sick man.

3. Could Jesus forgive sins?

   Yes, Jesus had power to forgive sins.

Bible Verse to Learn

"Jesus saw their faith." Mark 2:5

43. The Sick Man at the Pool

In the city of Jerusalem, there was a special pool. Sometimes an angel went down into the pool and stirred the water. Then whoever stepped into the water first would be healed, no matter what kind of sickness he had.

Around the pool lay many sick people. Some were blind, some were crippled, and some were helpless. They were waiting for the water to move.

One day Jesus came near the pool. He saw the sick people. One man had been sick for thirty-eight years. Jesus asked him, "Would you like to be made well?"

The man said sadly, "Sir, I have no one to help me. Someone else always steps into the water before me."

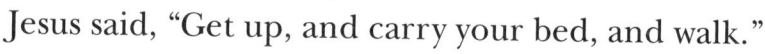

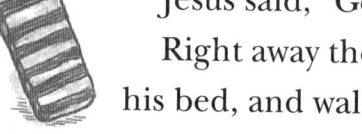

Jesus said, "Get up, and carry your bed, and walk."

Right away the man was healed. He got up, picked up his bed, and walked away.

Soon some Jews saw him carrying his bed. It was the Sabbath Day. The Jews said, "You should not be carrying your bed today."

The man answered, "The person who healed me told me to carry my bed with me."

The Jews asked, "Who is the man who healed you?"

The man did not know who had healed him. Jesus had gone away from him into the crowd of people.

Later Jesus met the man in the temple. Jesus said, "Do not sin anymore, or something worse may happen."

Now the man knew that Jesus had healed him. He went to the Jews. He told them, "Jesus made me well."

The Jews were angry because Jesus did a wonderful thing on the Sabbath Day. They wanted to kill Jesus.

Jesus said to the Jews, "God is My Father. My Father loves Me and gives Me power. You should read the Scriptures. Moses and the prophets wrote about Me. You do not have the love of God in your hearts, or you would believe the Scriptures and the words I say."

Jesus loved the Jews. He wanted all men to believe Him and love God. Jesus wanted to do what pleased God.

Questions and Answers

1. Why did the water in the pool move sometimes?

     An angel came and stirred the water in the pool.

2. Did the man know who had healed him?

     No, the man did not know at first.

3. What day did Jesus heal this man?

     Jesus healed the man on the Sabbath Day.

Bible Verse to Learn

"Search the scriptures." John 5:39

44. A Storm Obeys Jesus

As Jesus went from place to place, great crowds of people followed Him. Many people came to hear Him teach.

One day Jesus and His disciples sat on the side of a mountain. Many people could see and hear Jesus. He taught them a long time. He said, "You will be happy if you obey God. Love and pray for those who hate you. Trust God to take care of you. See the birds and the pretty flowers. God takes care of them each day. God loves and cares for you too."

Jesus also told the people to be wise. Jesus said, "If you obey My words, you will be like the wise man, who built his house upon a rock. Do not be like the foolish man, who built his house upon the sand. When the storm came, his house fell down."

Another day Jesus told a story about the man who planted seeds. The birds ate some seeds. Some plants did not grow well on the stony ground or where thorns were growing. But some plants grew up and had good fruit. Jesus said, "If you obey the Bible, you will be like the good ground. You will have good fruit for God." Jesus told other stories too. He wanted to help the people understand His true message of love.

That same evening, after the people went home, Jesus and His disciples got into a ship. Jesus was tired from the busy day. Soon He was fast asleep on a pillow in the ship.

Out on the water, the wind began to make big waves. The waves made water come into the ship. It was a bad storm. The disciples were afraid. They woke Jesus. They said, "Master, we are sinking!"

Jesus stood up. He spoke to the wind and the sea. He said, "Peace, be still." The wind stopped at once. The water was calm.

Jesus asked His disciples, "Why were you afraid?"

The disciples were even more afraid. How great was Jesus' power! Even the wind and the sea obeyed Him.

Questions and Answers

1. Should we be like the wise or the foolish man?

   We should be like the wise man.

2. What did Jesus say to the wind and the sea?

   Jesus said, "Peace, be still."

3. Did the wind and the sea obey Jesus?

   Yes, the wind stopped, and the water was calm.

Bible Verse to Learn

"We trust in the living God." 1 Timothy 4:10

45. The Daughter of Jairus

One time when Jesus healed a man, the man wanted to go with Jesus. But Jesus said, "Go back to your home. Tell others about the great things God did for you."

The man obeyed. When Jesus came back to that city, many people were waiting for Him. They were glad to see Jesus.

One man named Jairus came and fell at Jesus' feet. He said, "Please come to my house and heal my only daughter. She is so sick that she may die."

Jesus started to walk to Jairus' house. A crowd of people went with Jesus. In the crowd was a woman who was sick for twelve years. She had gone to doctors and had spent all her money, but she only grew worse. Now she thought, "If I can only touch Jesus' clothes, I will be healed." So she came close to Jesus and touched the hem of His robe. Right away she was healed.

Jesus turned and asked, "Who touched Me?"

Peter and others said, "Master, many people are walking close to You. Anyone could easily touch You."

But Jesus said, "Someone touched Me on purpose because I felt healing power go from Me."

The woman was afraid. She came and told Jesus what had happened. Jesus said, "Be of good comfort. Because you had faith, you were healed."

At this same time, someone came to Jairus and said, "Your daughter is dead. Jesus will not need to come."

When Jesus heard it, He said to Jairus, "Do not be afraid. Believe in Me, and she will be healed."

Soon Jesus came to Jairus' house. The people were crying loudly. Jesus told them, "Do not cry. The girl is not dead. She is sleeping." The people laughed at Jesus. They did not believe Him.

Jesus had everyone leave the house except the father, the mother, and three disciples. Jesus took the girl's hand and said, "Stand up." Right away she got up and walked. How surprised and happy her parents were! Jesus could do wonderful things.

Questions and Answers

1. Did the woman touch Jesus' clothes or His hand?
   She touched Jesus' clothes.

2. Did Jesus know someone had touched His clothes?
   Yes, Jesus knew someone had touched His clothes.

3. Did Jesus get to Jairus' house too late?
   No, Jesus made Jairus' daughter alive and well.

Bible Verse to Learn

"The people gladly received him." Luke 8:40

46. Jesus Feeds Many People

Jesus and His disciples had heard that the king killed John the Baptist. Now they wanted to be alone and rest. So they went in a boat across the lake.

But the people heard where Jesus had gone. Great crowds walked around the lake to come to Jesus. Jesus had pity on them. He healed many sick ones. He taught the people a long time.

At last the disciples told Jesus to send the people away. But Jesus said, "Before they go away, you should give them food to eat."

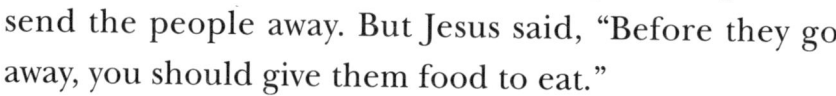

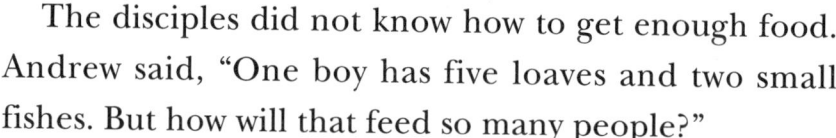

The disciples did not know how to get enough food. Andrew said, "One boy has five loaves and two small fishes. But how will that feed so many people?"

Jesus said, "Tell everyone to sit down." So the people sat on the grass. There were about five thousand men. There were many women and children too.

Jesus took the boy's lunch. He gave thanks to God. Then Jesus broke the loaves and gave the pieces of food to His disciples. They gave the food to the people. They kept giving food until everyone had enough to eat.

Jesus said, "Pick up all the pieces that are left."

The disciples gathered twelve baskets of food.

Then Jesus sent the people away. He told His disciples to go in the boat. But Jesus went to a mountain to pray.

That night Jesus saw the disciples out on the water. The wind was blowing, and the waves rocked the boat.

Jesus went to them. He was walking on the water.

When the disciples saw Him, they were afraid. Jesus said, "Be of good cheer. It is I. Do not be afraid."

Peter said, "Let me come to You on the water."

Jesus said, "Come."

So Peter got out of the boat. He walked on the water. But when he saw the waves, he began to sink. He cried, "Lord, save me!" Jesus reached out His hand to Peter.

When Jesus and Peter got into the boat, the wind stopped. All the disciples worshiped Jesus. They said, "Truly You are the Son of God."

Questions and Answers

1. How much food did Jesus use to feed the people?
   Jesus used five loaves and two small fishes.

2. Who walked on the water on the lake?
   Jesus and Peter walked on the water.

3. Who did the disciples say Jesus is?
   They said Jesus is the Son of God.

Bible Verse to Learn

"Thou art the Son of God." Matthew 14:33

47. The Kind Samaritan

One time a lawyer asked Jesus, "Master, what should I do to get to heaven?"

Jesus asked the lawyer, "What does the Law of God say?"

The man said, "We should love the Lord with all our heart, with all our strength, and with all our mind. We should love our neighbor as much as we love ourselves."

Jesus said, "Your answer is right. Do this, and you will please God."

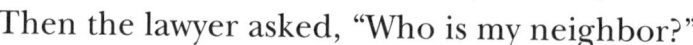

Then the lawyer asked, "Who is my neighbor?"

To answer his question, Jesus told a story. Jesus said, "One time a man walked alone from Jerusalem to Jericho. At one place some thieves caught him. They took away his clothes. They hurt him very badly. Then they quickly went away. The man was left lying by the side of the road. He was too hurt to move.

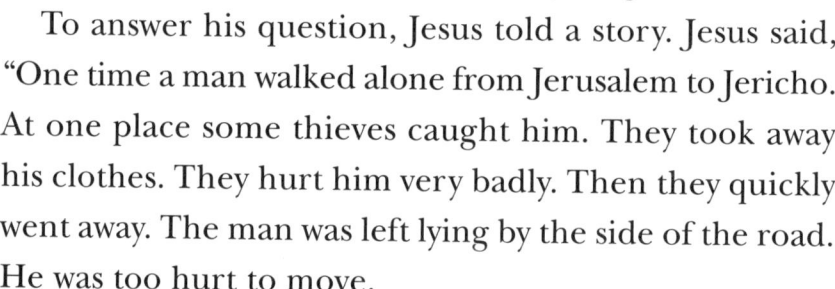

"Soon a priest came by. He saw the wounded man, but he did not go close to him. He stayed on the other side of the road and went on his way.

"Next a Levite came to the place where the poor man lay. The Levite looked at the man, but did not help him either. The Levite also went on down the road.

"At last a man from Samaria came near. The Samaritan saw the poor, hurt man. The Samaritan felt sorry for him. He poured oil and wine into the man's wounds. He bound his wounds with clean cloth. He put the man on his own donkey and took him to an inn. The Samaritan stayed with the wounded man all night and took care of him.

"The next morning, the Samaritan went to the master of the inn. He gave him money and said, 'Take care of this wounded man. If you need more money, I will pay you more when I come again.' "

Now Jesus asked the lawyer, "Which of the three men acted like a neighbor to the man who was hurt?"

The lawyer answered, "The man who helped him."

Jesus said, "Go and do as he did." Jesus wants everyone to be kind to others. This pleases God.

Questions and Answers

1. How did the man get hurt?

   Some thieves hurt him very badly.

2. Which man stopped and helped the poor man?

   The Samaritan stopped and helped him.

3. Can we still hear the stories Jesus told?

   Yes, we can hear the stories from the Bible.

Bible Verse to Learn

"Thou shalt love thy neighbour." Mark 12:31

48. Mary, Martha, and Lazarus

Mary and Martha and their brother Lazarus lived in Bethany. They loved Jesus.

One day when Jesus came to their house, Martha had so much work to do. But Mary sat down and listened to Jesus' words.

Martha wished her sister, Mary, would help her. She said to Jesus, "Lord, don't You care if I must do all the work? Please tell Mary to help me."

Jesus spoke kindly, "Martha, Martha, you are worried about your work. But Mary is doing something better. She is listening to My words of truth from God."

Another time Lazarus was sick. Mary and Martha sent a message to Jesus. After Jesus heard that Lazarus was sick, He stayed where He was two more days. Then Jesus and His disciples came to Bethany. Already Lazarus was in his grave four days.

Friends were staying with Mary and Martha to comfort them. Someone told Martha that Jesus was coming, so she went to meet Him. She said, "Lord, if You would have been here, Lazarus would not have died."

Jesus told Martha, "Your brother shall become alive."

She said, "Yes, Lord, I know that he will be alive in the resurrection at the end of time."

Jesus said, "I have power to give life now on earth. Also, those who believe in Me will never die in heaven. Do you believe this?"

Martha answered, "Yes, Lord, I believe You."

Then Martha went and brought Mary to Jesus. Together they walked to the cave where Lazarus was buried. Many friends went with them. Jesus saw all the people weeping because they were so sad. Jesus loved them. Jesus wept.

At the cave was a big stone. Jesus said, "Take the stone away." Then Jesus prayed. He thanked God.

Jesus said, "Lazarus, come out." And Lazarus came out of the cave. He was alive! Jesus could do great things. Many of the people who saw what Jesus had done believed that Jesus is the Saviour sent from God.

Questions and Answers

1. What did Mary do while Martha worked?
   Mary listened to Jesus' words.

2. How many day was Lazarus in his grave?
   Lazarus was in his grave four days.

3. Did Jesus love Mary and Martha and the friends?
   Yes, Jesus loved all the people.

Bible Verse to Learn
"Jesus wept." John 11:35

49. God Loves Every Person

One day Jesus told stories about things that were lost.

Jesus said, "People are happy when lost things are found. The angels in heaven are happy too when people are saved from sin."

One story Jesus told was about the sheep. A shepherd had one hundred sheep. He took good care of them. But one day he counted only ninety-nine sheep.

"I must go find my one lost sheep," thought the shepherd. So away he went. He kept looking and looking. Where could it be?

At last he found the one lost sheep. Then he carried it home. He said to his friends, "Be happy with me because I have found my sheep that was lost."

Another story was about the woman who had ten pieces of silver. When she lost one piece, she lit a candle and swept the floor. She kept hunting until she had found it. She also told her friends, "Now we can be happy. I have found my lost piece of silver."

The last story was about a father who had two sons. The younger one said, "Father, give me the money that you are keeping for me." So the father gave his money to his two sons.

The younger son took his money and went far away. There he wasted his money. He did whatever he wanted to do. But he was not happy. He was very poor and sad.

One day he thought about his father. He said, "I will go home. I will tell my father I am sorry. I will stay at home and work for my father."

So the son went home. His father saw him coming. His father ran to meet him. How happy the father was to see his lost son at last!

Jesus told these stories long ago. But He wants us to read them too. Jesus wants everyone to know of God's great love. God loves every person just like the father loved his lost son. God wants people to be sorry when they do wrong things. God wants everyone to be happy and to love God. God wants everyone to obey the Bible.

Questions and Answers

1. How many sheep were lost?

    One sheep was lost.

2. Was the woman happy or sad to find her silver?

    The woman was happy.

3. Was the younger son sorry he had done wrong?

    Yes, he was sorry he had done wrong.

Bible Verse to Learn

"Rejoice in the Lord alway." Philippians 4:4

50. The Ten Lepers

One day as Jesus was going to the next village, ten men saw Him. The ten men had a terrible disease called leprosy. No doctor could help them get well. They had to stay away from other people so no one else would get the terrible disease from them.

The ten men believed Jesus could help them. They stayed far away from Jesus. They called loudly, "Jesus, Master, have mercy on us." They watched to see if Jesus heard them.

Jesus heard their call. He saw them standing far away. Jesus said, "Go show yourselves to the priests."

This was what the Law said. If someone had leprosy and got well, they had to go to the priest. The priest had to see that they did not have any leprosy before they could go back to live with their families again.

The ten men obeyed Jesus. They started to go to the priest right away. As they went, they were healed. Their bodies did not have leprosy anymore.

One of them saw that he was healed. He was so happy! He wanted to thank Jesus. He turned around and came back. He fell at Jesus' feet. He gave glory to God.

Jesus said, "Weren't there ten men that were healed? Where are the nine? Only one is giving glory to God."

Jesus told the man at His feet, "Arise, and go on your way. Your faith has healed you."

Jesus is glad when people give glory to God. Jesus wants everyone to be thankful for God's help.

One time Jesus told a story about two men who went into the temple to pray. One man was proud. He prayed, "God, I thank You that I am not like the men who sin. I do good deeds. I give money to the poor people."

The other man stood alone. His heart was sad. He prayed, "God, have mercy on me and forgive my sins."

Jesus said, "God heard the prayer of the humble man. God forgave him. God is pleased when people give glory to God. But God does not answer the proud. God is not pleased when people think they do not need God."

Questions and Answers

1. How many men with leprosy did Jesus heal?
   Jesus healed ten men with leprosy.

2. How many came back to thank Jesus?
   One man came back and thanked Jesus.

3. Does God hear the prayers of the proud or the humble?
   God hears the prayers of the humble people.

Bible Verse to Learn

"Humble yourselves in the sight of the Lord." James 4:10

51. Jesus Blesses the Children

Jesus loves all people. He loves the old and the young. He loves the sick and the healthy. He loves the poor and the rich. Jesus is always kind to everyone.

One day some mothers brought their little children to Jesus. They wanted Jesus to touch their children. But the disciples did not want the children to bother Jesus. They told the mothers, "Take your children away."

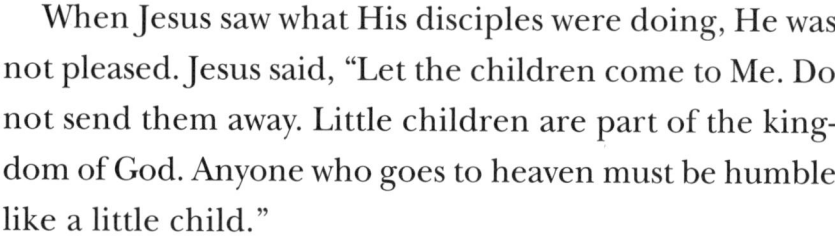

When Jesus saw what His disciples were doing, He was not pleased. Jesus said, "Let the children come to Me. Do not send them away. Little children are part of the kingdom of God. Anyone who goes to heaven must be humble like a little child."

Then Jesus took the little children in His arms. He placed His hands on others. He blessed the children.

The mothers were glad Jesus loved their children. The children were glad to be close to Jesus.

Soon after this, Jesus and His disciples started to go to Jerusalem. As they walked, He said, "When we get to Jerusalem, I will need to suffer." Jesus knew what was going to happen. Jesus wanted His disciples to love and trust God no matter what happened.

On the way to Jerusalem, Jesus and His disciples went through Jericho. Not far from the city, a large crowd of people followed them. At the side of the road sat a blind man. He wondered why he heard so many people walking. Someone told him, "Jesus is passing by."

The blind man had heard about Jesus. He cried loudly, "Jesus, have mercy on me!" Other people told the blind man to be quiet, but he cried out still more.

Jesus stopped. He told them to bring the blind man. Jesus asked, "What do you want Me to do for you?"

The blind man answered, "Lord, I would like to see."

Jesus said, "Go on your way. Your faith has healed you." Right away the man could see. He followed Jesus and gave glory to God. All the people around him also praised God. Jesus wanted people to give God praise.

Questions and Answers

1. Did Jesus love all the little children?
   Yes, Jesus loved and blessed the children.

2. Did Jesus love the blind man?
   Yes, Jesus made the blind man see.

3. What did all the people do?
   All the people praised God.

Bible Verse to Learn

"Praise ye the Lord." Psalm 150:1

52. Zacchaeus Climbs a Tree

Many, many people were walking with Jesus. One man named Zacchaeus was not very tall. He wanted to see Jesus, but the crowd was too big.

Zacchaeus had an idea. He ran ahead of the crowd. He climbed up into a sycamore tree. Then he waited and watched for the crowd to come by that way.

Jesus and all the people came closer. At the tree, Jesus stopped. He looked up. Jesus said to Zacchaeus, "Zacchaeus, come down quickly. I must come to your house today."

So Zacchaeus quickly came down. Zacchaeus was very happy. He wanted Jesus to come to his house.

Some people in the crowd did not like Zacchaeus. They said he was a sinner because he was a rich tax collector. They thought he made the people pay too much money.

Now Zacchaeus stood before Jesus. Zacchaeus said, "Lord, I want to give half of the things I own to the poor people. If I have taken any money from any person that was not right, I will give back four times as much."

Jesus said, "Today Zacchaeus has found salvation. I came to save everyone who is sorry he did wrong and who wants to do right."

Soon Jesus and His disciples came near Jerusalem. Jesus sent two of His disciples to a certain village. He said, "You will find a young donkey tied. Untie it, and bring it to Me. If anyone asks why you are taking the donkey, say, 'The Lord needs it.' "

The two disciples did as Jesus said. They found the donkey. They told the owners that Jesus needs it. They brought the donkey to Jesus. They put some clothes on the donkey's back. Then Jesus sat on it.

Now Jesus rode to Jerusalem. Many people walked ahead of Him. Many other people followed. Some people put clothes on the ground. Other people took branches from palm trees. The people were happy to see Jesus. They began to praise God and say, "Hosanna; Blessed is the King that cometh in the Name of the Lord."

Questions and Answers

1. Who climbed up into a tree?

   Zacchaeus climbed up into a tree.

2. Why did he climb up into a tree?

   Zacchaeus wanted to see Jesus.

3. What did Jesus ride on into Jerusalem?

   Jesus rode on a donkey.

Bible Verse to Learn

"Hosanna to the Son of David." Matthew 21:15

53. The Last Supper

At Jerusalem, Jesus went into the temple. The temple was a place to worship. But He saw people buying and selling animals for sacrifices. Jesus sent them all out. He said, "God's house should be a place of prayer." The people could do their work outside the temple.

Then the blind and the lame came into the temple to Jesus. Jesus loved and healed them.

The leaders of the Jews were not pleased that Jesus did such wonderful things. The leaders heard the children praising God in the temple and saying, "Hosanna." The leaders wanted the children to be quiet.

But Jesus said, "The Scriptures say that from the lips of little children, God gets perfect praise."

Jesus often talked to the leaders about the Scriptures. Jesus wanted them to believe the truth. But the leaders hated Jesus. They planned to kill Jesus.

Jesus also talked to His disciples. Jesus loved them. He told them about things that would happen at the end of the world. Jesus said His followers should be busy doing good until Jesus comes to take them to heaven.

One of the disciples named Judas Iscariot loved money more than he loved Jesus. He promised to help leaders catch Jesus. They promised to give Judas money.

Soon it was time to eat the Passover feast. Jesus' disciples got the meal ready in an upper room. It was the last supper Jesus ate with His disciples before He died. As they were eating, Jesus said, "One of you will help the leaders find Me to take Me away."

This made the disciples sad. One by one they asked, "Is it I?" They loved Jesus. They did not want Jesus to be killed. But Judas knew what he had promised to do.

Jesus gave bread to the disciples to eat. He gave them grape juice to drink. After supper He washed their feet. Jesus said, "I want you to do as I showed you. You will be happy if you obey My words." Jesus taught them a long time. Then they sang a hymn.

Questions and Answers

1. What did the children say in the temple?
   The children said, "Hosanna," and praised God.

2. What did Jesus and His disciples do in the upper room?
   They ate the Last Supper, or the Passover feast.

3. Did Jesus wash their feet or their hands?
   Jesus washed their feet.

Bible Verse to Learn
"I have given you an example." John 13:15

54. Jesus Died on the Cross

It was dark and late. Jesus and His disciples left the upper room. They went out to a garden.

Jesus told His disciples they would all leave Him that night. But they said they would not leave Him. Jesus was their best Friend. They loved Jesus.

In the garden, Jesus said, "Stay here while I go on to pray."

Three times, Jesus prayed, "O My Father, Thy will be done." Jesus was in great sorrow. An angel came to help Him.

Three times, Jesus came back to His disciples. They were sleeping each time. Jesus woke them. He told them to watch and pray. The enemies were coming soon.

Suddenly a crowd of men with swords were there. Judas was with them. Judas kissed Jesus. Other men quickly held Jesus. Jesus did not try to get away.

Peter wanted to save Jesus. He cut off a man's ear with a sword. But Jesus touched the ear and healed it.

The enemies took Jesus with them. The disciples were afraid. They ran away just like Jesus had said they would.

The men took Jesus to the high priest. Some people told lies about Jesus. They spit on Him. They hit Him.

They took Jesus to Pilate. They said Jesus should die.

Pilate asked Jesus, "Are You the King of the Jews?"

Jesus said, "I came to be a king to all people who will hear the truth."

Pilate said, "This man is not bad. Let Him go free."

But the enemies and the crowd of people shouted, "Crucify Him! Crucify Him!" Then the soldiers hurt Jesus. They put a crown of thorns on His head. Pilate let them take Jesus out on a hill to be crucified.

They nailed Jesus on a cross between two thieves. One thief believed Jesus. He was sorry for his sins. Jesus said, "Today you will be with Me in heaven."

As Jesus hung on the cross, the land was dark in the afternoon. When Jesus died, there was an earthquake. One of the soldiers who saw the things that happened said, "Truly this was the Son of God."

Questions and Answers

1. What did Jesus pray in the garden?
   "O My Father, Thy will be done."

2. What did the crowd of people shout?
   "Crucify Him! Crucify Him!"

3. What did Jesus hang on when He died?
   Jesus hung on a cross.

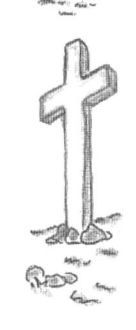

Bible Verse to Learn
"Thy will be done." Matthew 26:42

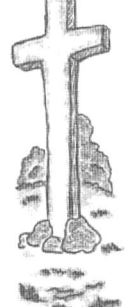

55. Jesus Goes Back to Heaven

Joseph and Nicodemus wanted to bury Jesus. Pilate said they may. So they took Jesus' body off the cross. They laid Jesus' body in a new tomb. For a door, they used a great big stone.

The next day was the Sabbath Day. Jesus' friends rested.

But early on the first day of the next week, some women came to Jesus' grave. They did not know who would roll away the big stone.

But when the women came to the grave, the stone was already rolled away! A shining angel from heaven had rolled the stone away and sat on it.

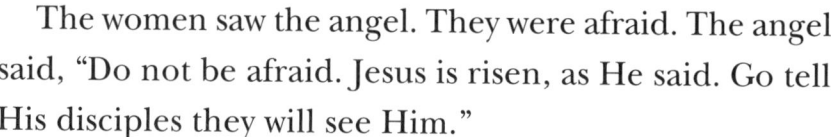

The women saw the angel. They were afraid. The angel said, "Do not be afraid. Jesus is risen, as He said. Go tell His disciples they will see Him."

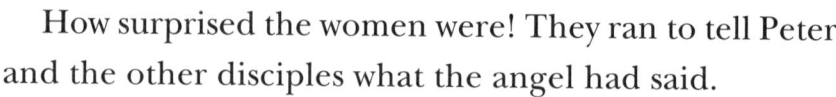

How surprised the women were! They ran to tell Peter and the other disciples what the angel had said.

When Peter and John heard this, they ran to the grave. They saw the grave was empty. So they went home. But Mary Magdalene did not go home. She stood outside the grave, crying. Soon Jesus came. He talked to Mary. How happy Mary must have been!

That same day, Jesus walked with two of His friends. He talked with them, but they did not know it was Jesus. They thought He was a stranger. After He left, they knew it was Jesus. Their hearts were so happy.

Jesus stayed on earth forty days after He arose. Jesus appeared to His disciples many times. He did special things. He went through closed doors without opening them. Jesus is the Son of God.

One day Jesus talked with His disciples. He blessed them. While Jesus was speaking, He began to rise from the ground. Higher and higher Jesus went. Soon He went into a cloud. He was going back to heaven. The disciples could not see Jesus anymore.

Two angels came and said, "Jesus will come again just like you saw Him go away." Then the disciples worshiped. They went to Jerusalem with happy hearts.

Questions and Answers

1. Who rolled away the big stone?
   An angel rolled away the big stone.

2. What special thing did Jesus do?
   Jesus went through closed doors.

3. Where did Jesus go in the cloud?
   Jesus went to heaven in a cloud.

Bible Verse to Learn

"He is risen, as he said." Matthew 28:6

56. Peter Has Power to Heal

The disciples stayed together at Jerusalem. They remembered the words Jesus had taught them.

Ten days after Jesus went to heaven, Peter preached to a big crowd of people. All the people listened to Peter. Peter preached that Jesus is the Saviour.

Many people believed what Peter preached. The people asked Peter, "What shall we do?"

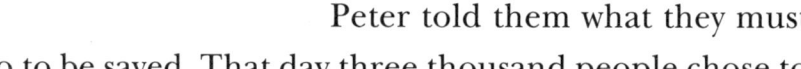

Peter told them what they must do to be saved. That day three thousand people chose to obey God. They believed the truth and were baptized. The church was growing larger.

God gave the disciples power to do special things. One afternoon Peter and John went to the temple to pray. A lame man sat at the gate of the temple. The lame man was begging for money. Peter stopped and talked to the lame man. Peter said, "I do not have any money. But I will give you what I do have. In the Name of Jesus, stand up and walk." Peter had power from God.

Right away the man jumped up. He went with Peter and John into the temple. He was walking and leaping and praising God. He was not lame anymore.

Another time Peter visited a sick man. For eight years, the man had needed to stay in bed. Peter said, "Jesus makes you well. Get up and make your bed." Right away the man got up. He was healed by God's power.

Soon after this, a woman named Dorcas died. She had been kind to many poor people. Her church friends sent two men to ask Peter to come to them.

When Peter came, many widows were crying in the room where Dorcas' body lay. The poor mothers showed Peter the coats and clothes Dorcas had made for them.

Then Peter told everyone to go out of the room. Peter kneeled down and prayed. He said to the body, "Dorcas, get up." Right away Dorcas opened her eyes and sat up.

How thankful the friends and poor widows were! Many people believed in God when they heard how God had made Dorcas alive. God's power is very great and wonderful.

Questions and Answers

1. What did the lame man beg for?

   The lame man begged for money.

2. What did Peter do for the lame man?

   Peter healed the lame man by God's power.

3. Who became alive after Peter prayed?

   Dorcas became alive after Peter prayed.

Bible Verse to Learn

"Many believed in the Lord." Acts 9:42

57. The Church Prays for Peter

Peter was in prison. The king planned to kill Peter because Peter preached about Jesus. The enemies did not want Peter to preach about Jesus.

The church kept praying for Peter. They wanted Peter to be faithful even if he must die.

The night before Peter was to be killed, something wonderful happened. Peter was fast asleep between two soldiers. Chains were on Peter's hands. Guards stood at the prison doors.

Suddenly an angel appeared. A light shone. The angel awoke Peter and said, "Get up quickly." The chains fell off Peter's hands. The angel told Peter, "Put on your sandals and your coat, and follow me."

Peter followed the angel out of the prison. It was so wonderful that Peter thought he was dreaming. When the angel and Peter came to the iron gate, it opened by itself. Peter and the angel walked through the open gate and down the street. Then the angel disappeared.

Peter was alone. He said to himself, "Now I am sure this is real. God sent his angel to save me. I will go to John Mark's house. His house is not far away."

At John Mark's house, many Christians were praying.  Peter knocked at the gate. A girl named Rhoda came to open the gate. When she heard Peter's voice, she was so happy she did not open the gate. She ran into the house and said, "Peter is here!"

The other people did not believe her. But she was sure it was Peter. So they said, "It must be his angel."

All this time, Peter stood outside. Peter knocked at the gate again and again. Finally someone opened the gate. There stood Peter! How surprised everyone was! Peter told them that God had sent an angel to save him. Peter said, "Go tell the other Christians how God saved me." Then Peter went away to another place.

The next morning, the king sent his men to bring Peter out of prison. But the soldiers could not find Peter. God took care of Peter and kept him safe.

Questions and Answers

1. Who led Peter out of prison?

   An angel of God led Peter out of prison.

2. What were the Christians doing at John Mark's house?

   The Christians were praying.

3. Could the soldiers find Peter?

   No, the soldiers could not find Peter.

Bible Verse to Learn

"Pray without ceasing." 1 Thessalonians 5:17

58. Paul Preaches and Travels

A young man named Saul hated the Christians. He put them in prison. He hurt them too. Many Christians were afraid of Saul.

One day Saul was on the road to Damascus. Suddenly a bright light shone. Saul heard Jesus' voice. After this, Saul was blind. He was led into the city.

God sent Ananias to talk to Saul. He healed Saul's eyes. Saul became a Christian. He was baptized. Saul became a preacher too. He preached about Jesus. The people were surprised. Some Christians were still afraid of Saul. But Saul wanted to help the Christians now. He did not hurt them anymore.

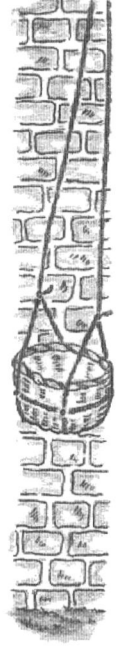

Saul's old friends did not want Saul to change. They tried to kill Saul. Christian friends helped Saul to get away from the enemies. One time they let Saul down over a wall in a basket so he could go away.

One day Saul was praying with the church at Antioch. The Holy Spirit said, "Send Barnabas and Saul away to do the work I have called them to do." God wanted them to go to other cities and preach about Jesus. So the ministers sent Barnabas and Saul away as God had said.

Saul's name was changed to Paul. Paul and Barnabas traveled to many cities. Everywhere they went, they told people about Jesus. They wanted people to know the truth.

Paul loved to help other people become Christians. When Paul came back from one trip, he went on another trip. He visited the new churches and helped them.

Sometimes people were angry with Paul. In one city, Paul and Silas were beaten and put into prison. They sang at midnight. Suddenly there was an earthquake. All the prison doors came open. The prison keeper was afraid. But Paul said, "Do not be afraid." Paul helped the keeper and his family to become Christians.

At Troas, Paul preached until midnight. A young man was sitting in a window. The young man went to sleep. He fell down to the ground and died. God helped Paul make the young man alive. God helped Paul many times.

Questions and Answers

1. Did Paul always help the Christians?

   No, Paul hurt them when he was a young man.

2. Did Paul stay in one place all the time?

   No, Paul traveled to many different places.

3. What did Paul and Silas do in prison at midnight?

   Paul and Silas sang in the prison.

Bible Verse to Learn

"Paul preached unto them." Acts 20:7

59. Paul Writes Letters

Paul wanted to visit the new churches. He wanted to preach to them. He wanted to help them.

But Paul could not go to all the churches every time. So sometimes Paul sent other ministers to help the churches. Sometimes Paul wrote letters to tell the churches what to do.

God's Spirit told Paul what to write to the churches. So we know what Paul wrote is true.

Paul wrote many things. Paul wrote about Jesus. Jesus died on the cross to save people from sin. Jesus is in heaven now. Someday Jesus will come back to earth. The people who died will come out of their graves. All the people who loved and obeyed Jesus will meet Him in the air and live with Him in heaven forever.

Paul wrote about churches. The leaders should be good examples. The members should help each other and obey the leaders. The preachers should speak the language of the people so everyone can understand the message.

Paul wrote about homes. God wants homes to be happy. A man and woman who marry should love each other and live together until one dies. Parents should love and teach their children. Children should love and

obey their parents.

Men should be the leaders in the home and church. The women should listen to the men. The women should cover their hair with a veil to show they obey God's plan.

Sometimes Paul wrote about problems. Some Christians thought other Christians had done wrong. They wanted to go to the judge in court. But Paul said they should forgive each other and have peace.

Paul wrote letters to ministers too. Paul told Timothy and Titus to preach the truth and to keep the church pure.

Paul wrote to a master who had a slave. The slave ran away. Paul helped the slave become a Christian. Paul told the master to forgive his slave and treat the slave as a Christian brother.

Paul wanted men and women and children to love Jesus and to do right. This pleases God. It makes us happy too.

Questions and Answers

1. Who told Paul what to write in the letters?
   God's Spirit told Paul what to write.

2. What should children do in their homes?
   Children should love and obey their parents.

3. Should men or women be the leaders?
   Men should be the leaders.

Bible Verse to Learn

"Hear the word of God, and do it." Luke 8:21

60. Our Happy Home in Heaven

Jesus went back to heaven. He promised to prepare a home for all who love and obey Him.

Someday He is coming in the clouds. Everyone will see Him. He will take His people home to heaven to live with Him forever.

Jesus' disciples preached what Jesus had taught them. But the enemies did not want the disciples to preach about Jesus. The enemies put John on an island alone so he could not preach to any people. But God was with John.

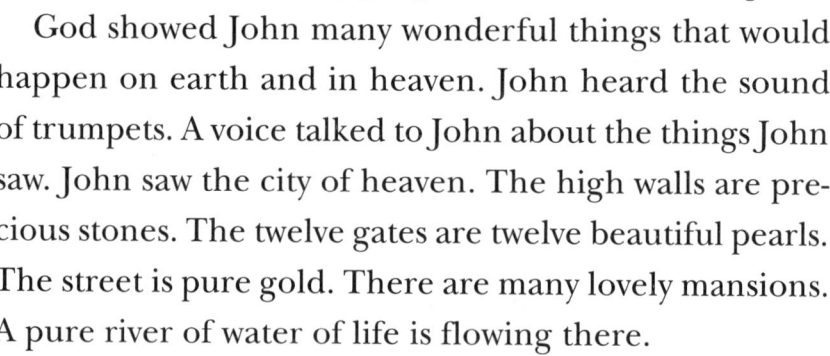

God showed John many wonderful things that would happen on earth and in heaven. John heard the sound of trumpets. A voice talked to John about the things John saw. John saw the city of heaven. The high walls are precious stones. The twelve gates are twelve beautiful pearls. The street is pure gold. There are many lovely mansions. A pure river of water of life is flowing there.

John saw many angels and many, many people around God's throne in heaven. The people wore white robes. They praised and worshiped God.

There is no temple in heaven because God is there. Everyone worships God. There is no sun to shine because

God's glory is the light. God's glory is always shining, so there is no night in that beautiful city.

Heaven is a very wonderful place. No sin is in heaven. Everyone will do what pleases God. There is no sorrow or tears. Jesus makes everyone happy. There is no pain. Everyone has a new body that will never get hurt or die.

On earth people die. All children who die will go to heaven. All the people who are saved from sin will go to heaven. Their names are written in God's Book of Life.

The people who do not love and obey Jesus will not go to heaven. They will go to hell forever. Hell is a terrible place. Bad Satan will be there. There is fire and pain. There is sadness and darkness.

Jesus wants people on earth to be ready and watching for Him. Jesus said, "Surely I will come quickly."

John said, "Even so, come, Lord Jesus."

Questions and Answers

1. Where did the enemies put John?

   The enemies put John on an island alone.

2. Why is there no sun to shine in heaven?

   God's glory is the light of heaven.

3. Will anyone be sad in heaven?

   No, everyone will be happy with Jesus.

Bible Verse to Learn

"God is in heaven." Ecclesiastes 5:2